From Vision to Action

FROM VISION TO ACTION

Remaking the World Through Social Entrepreneurship

JOHN MARKS

Columbia University Press
New York

Columbia University Press
Publishers Since 1893
New York   Chichester, West Sussex
cup.columbia.edu

Library of Congress Cataloging-in-Publication Data
Names: Marks, John, 1943– author.
Title: From vision to action : remaking the world through
social entrepreneurship / John Marks.
Description: New York : Columbia University Press, [2024] | Includes index.
Identifiers: LCCN 2024013006 | ISBN 9780231215572 (hardback) |
ISBN 9780231215589 (trade paperback) | ISBN 9780231560863 (ebook)
Subjects: LCSH: Social entrepreneurship. | Social change. | Social action.
Classification: LCC HD60 .M3654 2024 | DDC 338/.04—dc23/eng/20240328
LC record available at https://lccn.loc.gov/2024013006

Printed and bound by CPI Group (UK) Ltd, Croydon, CR0 4YY

Cover design: Noah Arlow
Cover images: Shutterstock

For Susan and Daniel

Let yourself be silently drawn by the strange pull of what you really love. It will not lead you astray.

—RUMI

Contents

Acknowledgments

First and foremost, I would like to thank Susan Collin Marks for loving me and for working as my partner for the last three decades. Susan read each draft chapter of this book and made hugely useful suggestions. Although I am ultimately responsible for the content, she is clearly the book's godmother.

I would also like to thank Shamil Idriss, my successor as CEO of Search, for his support and for his extraordinary contributions in leading the organization.

Others who are currently at Search—or who once were—allowed me to interview them about their memories of the work which we did together. These people made a substantial contribution, and they are listed in alphabetic order: Noufal Abboud, John Bell, Tom Dine, Eran Fraenkel, Mary Jacksteit, Dirk-Jan Koch, Stephanie Koury, Sandra Melone, Vilma Venkovska Milčev, Suheir Rasul, Sharon Rosen, Oussama Safa, Michael Shipler, Lisa Shochat, and Lena Slachmuijlder.

I also interviewed Ahmed Abaddi, Mohammed Belmahi, Emilio Cassinello, Theodore Kattouf, Allen Grossman, and Augustus Richard Norton. I thank them all—along with those who did not wish to be cited.

I would like to extend special thanks to Karen Zehr who served for fifteen years as Susan's and my loyal assistant. Indeed, Karen made an important contribution to this book when she suggested, as I was getting ready to step down from the leadership of Search, that she should make searchable scans of the many newsletters I had written over the years. I wouldn't have thought of this myself. However, when it came to actually writing the book, being easily able to find descriptions of incidents that took place up to thirty years ago proved invaluable in reconstructing events.

Craig Whitney, the longtime *New York Times* reporter and my friend since I was sixteen years old, graciously agreed to edit the first draft of the manuscript, and he did a great job. I am extremely grateful.

I send special thanks to Laurens Trimpe, my one-time squash partner who contributed excellent technical support.

I would also like to thank Myles Thompson, my editor at Columbia University Press, for choosing to publish the book and guiding me through the process. It had been 45 years since I had written an entire book, and Myles skillfully directed me on how to do it in these current times. He was ably assisted in this role by Brian Smith. Lastly, I would like to thank the project manager, Ben Kolstad, and the copyeditor, Kathryn Mikel, who did such a good job in clarifying my work.

Prologue

The year was 1989, and I was having dinner at a Holiday Inn overlooking the ocean in Santa Monica, California. At the table were William Colby, former director of the CIA; Ray Cline, former CIA deputy director; Feodor Sherbak, former deputy director of the KGB's Internal Security Directorate; Valentin Zvezdenkov, the KGB's former chief of counterterrorism and former *Rezident* in Cuba; and Igor Beliaev, a political observer with *Liternaturnaya Gazeta* (figure 0.1). The guest list reflected a major shift in my life.

Previously, I had been adversarial to my core, and I had written two books that revealed numerous abuses committed by the CIA. The first, coauthored with Victor Marchetti, was a bestseller; the second won a major award for investigative reporting. In the process, I had been highly critical of one of my dinner companions that night, William Colby. In *The CIA and the Cult of Intelligence*, I had described Colby's role in Vietnam in heading the notorious Phoenix and Counterterror programs that involved widespread torture and assassination. Then, in 1974, I had confronted Colby in front of a thousand people at a Washington, D.C. event at which he was the guest of honor. I had called him to account—and was shouted down—for the CIA's covert role in overthrowing the democratically elected government of Chile. And now here he was, fifteen years later, participating in a project I had organized to promote Soviet-American cooperation against

FIGURE 0.1 From left: Igor Beliaev, political observer, *Literaturnaya Gazeta*; Feodor Sherbak, former first deputy director, Internal Security Directorate, KGB; William Colby, former director, CIA; Ray Cline, former deputy director, CIA; Natalie Latter, interpreter; John Marks, president, Search for Common Ground; Valentin Zvezdenkov, former director of counterterrorism, KGB; and Oleg Proudkov, foreign editor, *Literaturnaya Gazeta*.

terror, and he was breaking bread with high-level retired KGB officers who had long been leaders of his *main enemy*. Although the Cold War was ending at the time of our dinner, dining with both the KGB and me must have been a bizarre experience for Colby.

We were in Santa Monica because the Rand Corporation has its headquarters in that city, and Rand was a partner in the current project. At least for me, working with Rand added to the incongruity because I had become a fierce critic of the Vietnam War, and Rand was seen as the primary think tank in support of American involvement in that war. Thus Rand had long been on my list of bad guys.

Clearly, everyone present that evening had at one time or another experienced profound differences with the other attendees. It was a dinner of strange bedfellows who had come together to see whether former enemies could find common ground around a shared concern—the prevention of terrorism.

Search for Common Ground[1] was the name of the nonprofit, non-governmental organization (NGO) I had founded seven years earlier to carry out projects like this one. Search had a very large vision: namely, to transform how the world dealt with conflict—starting with U.S.-Soviet relations—moving away from adversarial, *win-lose* approaches and toward nonadversarial, *win-win* problem-solving. I was convinced—and still am—that peace is possible and that even the most intractable conflicts can be resolved without violence.

Political activists usually define themselves by what they oppose, and I had been very much against the Vietnam War and the abuses committed by the CIA. However, my belief system had undergone considerable change by the time I sat down for dinner in Santa Monica. Having attended a series of human potential and personal growth workshops, I had begun to see grays in events that had once seemed to be either black or white. I had become aware that there was another way to work in the world. Instead of throwing monkey wrenches into the old system—at which I had become rather adept—I discovered that I wanted to build a new system. I had gradually dropped the need to be in opposition, although sometimes I still chose that option.

I had started to operate within the context of being *for* as opposed to being *against*. As an individual, I still had my own private views about which side in a conflict was more in the right and which was mostly wrong. But as a person dedicated to creating a peaceful world, I avoided getting caught up in divisive issues or favoring one party over the other. To have done so would have made me a participant in the conflict: part of the problem, not part of the solution. I wanted to work with contending parties to resolve disputes. With conflicts raging around the world, I was committed not to a particular outcome but to the process of finding common ground. PBS-TV host Jonathan Kwitny described my transition this way: "Marks moved from provocateur to peacemaker."

---

1. The organization was originally called the Nuclear Network, but a year later my colleagues and I decided to change the name to Search for Common Ground. It was familiarly known as "Search," and those of us who worked for it were often called "Searchers." These terms are used throughout the book. Search became one of the few NGOs in the world whose name described its method of operating. In essence, Searchers wore the organization's name on their sleeve.

When I founded Search in 1982, I had never heard the term *social entrepreneur*. In fact, beyond a few scholarly publications, the idea of social entrepreneurship had not yet come into wide usage. Bill Drayton, a pioneer in launching the field, happened to be a high school classmate of mine. The same year I started Search, Drayton launched Ashoka, a global network of social entrepreneurs that has grown to about 4,000 members, of which I later became one. Way back then, both Drayton and I headed much smaller operations. One day in 1983 I sought his advice about my fledgling organization. He listened as I described my vision and my approach, and then he informed me that I was a social entrepreneur. Not knowing exactly what he meant, I asked him to explain. He said that social entrepreneurs were innovative activists who created new initiatives, not for profit but to promote positive social change. That seemed to me to be an accurate job description of the role I wanted to play in leading Search. By telling me I was a social entrepreneur, Drayton made me feel like the Molière character who suddenly realizes that he has been speaking prose his whole life. I had been a social entrepreneur without knowing that I was one.

Before my meeting with Drayton, I had thought of myself as a *public interest advocate*. Subsequently, I began to describe myself as a social entrepreneur. Although this semantic switch did not appreciably alter the substance of my work, it provided me with an empowering framework, and I was able to move Search from a gleam in my eye into a global organization ready and able to promote social change.

By declaring that I was a social entrepreneur, I became a member of an international network of change makers. Most of my fellow social entrepreneurs were working on different kinds of issues, but we shared skills and tactics. Professionally we talked the same language and dealt with similar problems. We all enjoyed the extraordinary satisfaction that came from launching a new project, nurturing it, and seeing it blossom into an initiative that made the world a better place. I became convinced that significant change of the sort I and so many others yearned for would be far more likely to occur with substantial input from social entrepreneurs—nongovernmental pathfinders skilled at translating their vision into action.

My credentials as an activist social entrepreneur emerged from my hands-on experience in building Search from zero into the world's largest NGO involved in peace building. My partner and closest collaborator in this work was my wife, Susan Collin Marks. By the time we stepped down from Search's leadership in 2014, we had a staff of six hundred and offices

FIGURE 0.2 John Marks is presented with a Skoll Award for Social Entrepreneurship: (from left) Sally Osberg, Robert Redford, John Marks, Ben Kingsley, and Jeff Skoll.

in thirty-five countries. Our accomplishments were recognized by the Skoll Foundation, and they named us among its elite fellowship of social entrepreneurs (figure 0.2). In 2018, the work we initiated was nominated for the Nobel Peace Prize.

As a social entrepreneur, I was a self-taught practitioner—neither a theoretician nor a scholar. Over the years I developed a set of eleven working principles that formed the operational foundation for my work. These principles provide the basic structure of this book, and each is described in a separate chapter. The examples of how I applied each principle are drawn from my own experience. Here are summaries of the eleven principles.

1. **Start from vision.** Social entrepreneurs should have a clear sense of their vision, and everything they do should be in harmony with that vision—or at least should not be contrary to it.
2. **Be an applied visionary.** To be effective in changing the world, social entrepreneurs must be able to break down complicated tasks into finite, achievable pieces. They need to be incrementally transformational—or transformationally incremental.
3. ***"On s'engage, et puis on voit."*** This is a quote from Napoleon Bonaparte. A nonliteral translation is "one becomes engaged in an activity, and then

one sees new possibilities." Napoleon was a soldier by profession, and he was referring to military operations. His insight was that an attacking army needs to engage the enemy in order to understand the nature of its defenses. Similarly, social entrepreneurs have to be deeply engaged in their projects to discover innovative steps and approaches that they otherwise would not have seen.

4. **Keep showing up.** It has been said that "80 percent of success is showing up." For social entrepreneurs this means continuing to show up and avoiding dabbling or parachuting. Social entrepreneurs must commit themselves to long-term involvement in the projects that matter to them.

5. **Enroll credible supporters.** Because social entrepreneurs operate outside the proverbial box, they often are seen to be on the margins. Prominent backers are not indispensable but can be extremely helpful in moving forward their enterprises and initiatives.

6. **Expect the Dunbar Factor.** Social entrepreneurs need to be prepared to deal with high levels of complexity and uncertainty. When they intervene in what are almost always complex situations and systems, they are likely to face unanticipated problems, questions they did not think to ask, and unexpected outcomes.

7. **Make yesable propositions.** As Roger Fisher and William Ury wrote in their seminal book *Getting to Yes*, things work much better when people say "yes" to whatever is being proposed. Social entrepreneurs should be skilled at crafting proposals that are both in their interest and in the interest of the party to whom they are making the request.

8. **Practice aikido.** In the Japanese martial art of aikido, when someone is attacked, he or she does not try to reverse the assailant's energy flow by 180 degrees, as would be done in boxing (where the basic idea is to knock an attacker backward). In aikido, the person under attack accepts the attacker's energy, blends with it, and diverts it by ten or twenty degrees to make both people safe. For social entrepreneurs, this means accepting a conflict or a situation as it is and blending with it while transforming it one step at a time.

9. **Develop effective metaphors.** For social entrepreneurs, communicating compelling models and stories is a crucial aspect of being able to reframe reality. Most people will not shift their attitudes and behaviors if they do not have a realistic picture of where they are headed. An insightful metaphor or compelling story is often crucial in providing that picture.

10. **Display *chutzpah*.** *Chutzpah* is a Yiddish word for effrontery or audacity. Social entrepreneurs need to display sufficient nerve to push into difficult, risky situations but only in respectful and culturally appropriate ways. In other words, social entrepreneurs need to be politely pushy.

11. **Cultivate *Fingerspitzengefühl*.** This German word means having an intuitive sense of *knowing* at the tip of one's fingers. However, *fingerspitzengefühl* is not a quality that should be used in all cases to override rational thinking. Instead, when social entrepreneurs make decisions, they should factor in—but not be overwhelmed by—what feels right. The trick is to develop an appropriate mix of instinct and intellect.

This list of eleven principles has served me well, but I provide it with a word of caution: These principles are not absolute rules that must always be followed. They work most of the time, but sometimes they don't. I confess that there is not a principle among them that I have not violated on occasion because I felt something else was called for. Indeed, I strongly believe that social entrepreneurs should not follow any fixed methodology or ideology too closely; they are better served by displaying nimbleness and flexibility.

This book does not draw examples and stories from across the whole field of social entrepreneurship. Instead, I use my experiences at Search to illustrate how these underlying principles can be applied. My intention—and hope—is that readers will internalize the principles and employ them while adding insights gained from their own experience.

1

Start from Vision

Principle #1 of social entrepreneurship is "start from vision." A vision may appear in a flash or, as in my case, evolve from insights and experiences gained over many years. Social entrepreneurs need to have a clear sense of their vision—with the understanding that it is not set in concrete and that it may well change.

Individual social entrepreneurs almost always have different visions. Mine center on peace building, whereas other people deal with matters as varied as feeding the hungry, cleaning up the environment, or reforming the criminal justice system. These are all worthy causes. In this book, I focus on the processes and methodology involved in being a social entrepreneur rather than on the substance of various issues.

Social entrepreneurs should be able to boil down their vision into a few sentences easily articulated in what is often called an *elevator speech*. Above all, their vision needs to be authentic—not situational or transactional— reflect their essence, and be based on deeply held values. When social entrepreneurs reach the implementation stage, their actions should be consistent with their vision—or at least not be inconsistent with it. Once my core vision was in place, I was able to hold onto it for the next forty years, although I kept finding new ways to apply it.

My vision included ending—or at least improving—the adversarial relationship between the United States and the Soviet Union. Like so many people, I was terrified by the prospect of nuclear war during the Cold War period. I genuinely believed, as Jonathan Schell famously wrote, that the "fate of the earth" was at stake. If something profound was not done, I feared that the superpowers were likely to blow up the planet. Preventing nuclear war—in essence, saving the world—provided me with a huge amount of motivation. It still does. The best path I could see for reducing the threat was to move the superpowers from confrontation to cooperation. It was with that goal in mind that I worked in partnership with a Soviet colleague in 1989 to bring together in Santa Monica, California, former top officials of the CIA and the KGB (see prologue).

During the first years of Search for Common Ground, my approach did not reflect mainstream thinking among either hawks or doves. President Ronald Reagan had branded the Soviet Union (USSR) as the "Evil Empire," and most Americans seemed to believe that little or no common ground existed between the authoritarian Soviet regime and what was then called the Free World. But as the late Israeli prime minister Yitzhak Rabin would later say, "You don't make peace with friends."

I had come to believe that real security required transforming the very framework in which the United States and the USSR were opposing each other. I was convinced that there had to be better ways for the two countries to resolve their differences than interacting as perpetual enemies; neither could feel secure until they both felt secure. I became an advocate of what an international commission headed by Swedish Prime Minister Olof Palme called "common security." This concept reflected a very different—indeed, a transformational—way of dealing with security questions. The Palme Commission had declared that hostile, win-lose techniques were not only dangerous but in the end were ineffective and unworkable.

I have vivid memories of two incidents in which I failed to convince people on both sides of the political spectrum of the validity of my approach. The first occurred at a liberal Washington, D.C. think tank where arms control issues were being discussed. After listening to an interminable discussion of delivery systems, throw weights, and warheads, I saw an opening and thought perhaps I could get those present to see nuclear issues in a different context. My idea was to tell an insightful Sufi story I had first heard from my friend Abdul Aziz Said, a professor at the American University who was also a Sufi master.

The story describes a man who loses his keys as he walks down a street in the middle of the night. He is on his hands and knees underneath a streetlight looking for the keys when a second man comes along and offers to help. After a futile half-hour search, the second man says to the first, "Are you sure this is where you lost your keys?"

The first man replies, "No. I lost them across the street."

The second says, "So, why are we looking here?"

The first answers, "Because this is where the light is shining."

I felt that arms control had become the liberal opposition's center of attention because that was where the light was shining.

The think tankers reacted to my story with blank stares. What did losing keys have to do with arms control? There was virtually no recognition, despite my explanation, that I was calling for a paradigm shift regarding the U.S.-Soviet conflict and that arms control limitations would not in themselves solve the problem. I was moved, above all, by what Albert Einstein had said: "We shall require a substantially new manner of thinking if mankind is to survive."

My second instance of miscommunication occurred at the Council on Foreign Relations in Washington, D.C. I had secured an invitation to show a half-hour documentary film on *Common Security* that I had written for the TV series I was then producing for U.S. public TV stations. After watching my film, Cord Meyer, a hard-line Cold Warrior and retired CIA operator, declared, "I don't want to live in that kind of world."

Not only did my vision include living in that kind of world, but I was committed to helping to create it. I did not accept the premise that an adversarial relationship with the Soviet Union was inevitable. My work encompassed another possibility: namely, that peaceful, *win-win* solutions could be found for contentious problems—even those between the United States and the USSR.

I came to see that I needed to be able to share my vision in ways to which an audience could easily relate. This was particularly important for fund-raising purposes. Although I had the audacity to believe I could change the world, my good intentions alone were obviously not enough: I needed to be able to raise funds. This was a particularly difficult task during the first years when Search was still a tiny organization with only two employees, including me. In addition, I was told repeatedly that the name "Search for Common Ground" sounded flaky and that the organization had virtually no track record. As a result, established donors were reluctant to support us.

I made a virtue out of necessity and adopted what I called a *Tupperware* approach to fund-raising. That is, I stood up in living rooms and made what I hoped was a convincing pitch to sell my product. But I was not peddling pots and pans; I was sharing a vision of how to save the planet.

Somehow it worked, and Search was able to limp through those early years. Before I began, I had not understood that as the founder I was the "float" in the organization, that is, I was the only person willing to keep working even when there was not enough money to pay full salaries. In fact, I am not sure Search would have survived those rocky first days if my mother had not died during that period. As sad as I was about her passing, I was grateful that she left me a modest bequest in her will. My father, who was the soul of practicality, told me that I should invest the money in stocks and bonds and build a nest egg for the future. His advice came straight from being a youth during the Great Depression, when he had felt compelled to drop out of college to support his parents. I, on the other hand, was a creature of the post–World War II boom years, and to me everything seemed possible. With the money my mother left me, I decided that instead of buying securities, as my father advised, I would invest in my vision. My father said that this would cause me—as he so eloquently put it—"to piss away my inheritance." I ignored him, and as he predicted, within a few years all the money my mother left me was gone. I had spent it to make up the difference between the salary I was supposed to receive, which Search could not always afford, and the amount that I was actually paid. This turned out to be the best investment I ever made. I will always be grateful to my mother for making it possible. If the world were a fairer place, all social entrepreneurs would start with a similar nest egg, but that unfortunately is not the case. I was very lucky.

Concentrating as I was on the U.S.-Soviet conflict and the nuclear issue, I developed an easy-to-understand extended metaphor that I shared at Tupperware sessions to describe Search's approach. This became, in effect, my go-to metaphor. I asserted that the nuclear arms race between the superpowers was like two boys standing knee-deep in a room full of gasoline. One held ten matches; the other had seven. The boys were incessantly arguing over who had the most matches and who had the most explosive mix. To lessen the danger, the most common solution was to reduce the number of matches or to change the mix. In the real world, this was called arms control. For my part, I did not doubt that the mix and the quality of matches—that is, nuclear weapons—was important; that certain weapons were particularly perilous; that accidental ignition posed a huge threat; or that it would be destabilizing if one boy had too many matches or if the combination that he held provided a qualitative edge. However, I was much more concerned with the overall environment within which the boys were interacting. After all, they were standing knee-deep in gasoline, and one match could ignite everything.

Therefore, my primary interest was not to change the numbers or the mix but to drain the gasoline from the room—to shift the political climate or the paradigm within which the superpowers were confronting each other. I felt that the nuclear threat would not be lifted until the United States and the Soviet Union ended their win-lose, picking-at-scabs approach. For that to happen, the two sides needed to realize that they shared a common interest in cooperating and making the other feel secure. My metaphor of boys holding matches seemed to illustrate the need for transformation of the U.S.-Soviet relationship.

I recommend that social entrepreneurs develop extended metaphors, like this one, that embody their vision. Nevertheless, after the Cold War ended, I was never able to find a single metaphor that was equally encompassing. The best I could do was to devise mixed or multiple metaphors. These also proved to be effective, but they were much more difficult to articulate in an elevator.

Still, my gasoline-soaked imagery proved to be prophetic. Under the leadership of presidents Gorbachev and Reagan, the Soviet Union and the United States subsequently went through a profound transformation and greatly reduced the volatility of their relationship. Although their nuclear arsenals remained largely in place and the two countries retained the ability to destroy the earth, through the détente process nuclear war between them ceased to be an imminent threat. The superpowers stopped confronting each other as enemies. With a changed mindset toward the other in both countries, the threat that they would use their nukes mostly disappeared. At least in the beginning, the mix and number of matches did not change that much, but the environment in which the two countries faced each other became much less combustible. In essence, Reagan and Gorbachev were able to drain most of the gasoline from the room. Unfortunately, thirty-five years later, the confrontation surrounding the Ukraine War has resulted in large amounts of gasoline flooding back into the American-Russian relationship.

Nevertheless, the end of the Cold War confirmed my belief that even the most entrenched conflicts could be resolved without violence. I understood full well that this was an optimistic view, but then I am an optimist—which is probably a necessary quality for being a successful social entrepreneur. I certainly needed to be an optimist to start an organization called Search for Common Ground. I did not ignore the momentous problems that humanity faced, but I chose to see things as John Gardner, a former U.S. cabinet member and seminal thinker, saw them: "What we have before us are some breathtaking opportunities disguised as insoluble problems."

However, optimism alone is not enough. Like any social entrepreneur, I also needed to have the ability to make things happen. That was an important factor in both building an organization and launching new projects. If I had not believed I could contribute to meaningful social change, I probably would have chosen to lead a very different life. Instead, I stayed true to the idea that I could—and should—make a difference.

When people told me that something could not be done, I usually replied, "Let's find a way." Sometimes foolishly and sometimes wisely, I rejected the idea that most things were not possible. In some cultures, being told "no" absolutely means "no." In other places, and particularly to successful social entrepreneurs, refusing to take "no" for an answer is a useful quality— except on those occasions when it is not.

I tried to avoid being Pollyannaish, and I realized that events rarely moved forward on a predictable, straight-line basis. I found that the path of progress closely resembled a roller coaster—full of ups and downs. I admit that I very much preferred the ups, and I was confident that the overall thrust of human consciousness was moving in a positive direction. This optimistic belief was very much part of who I am—and of Search.

To implement our collective vision, my fellow Searchers and I almost certainly could not have acted alone as individuals. We needed the organizational base that Search gave us. To paraphrase Archimedes, Search provided a place to stand from which we could move the world—or at least try to do so. More generally, without an organization, social entrepreneurs usually cannot function in world-altering ways. As Jean Monnet, the founding father of the European Union, said, "Nothing changes without individuals. Nothing lasts without institutions."

After the U.S.-Soviet nuclear threat receded, my colleagues and I emphasized the prevention of violent conflict as a key part of our vision (figure 1.1). We noted that tens of millions of people worldwide were caught up in violence and, as a result, hundreds of thousands, if not millions, were dying every year. Violence shattered lives. It blocked development, and it almost always devastated the environment. In short, we Searchers believed that global

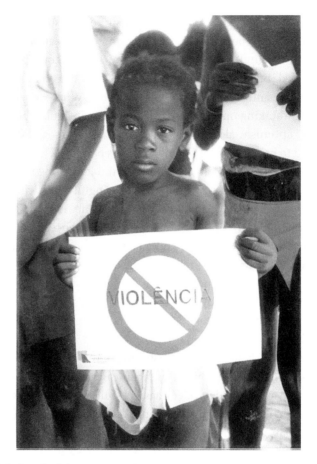

FIGURE 1.1 Search violence prevention poster.

problems were simply too complex and interconnected to be settled on a violent, adversarial basis.

We operated from the premise that the earth was running out of space, resources, and recuperative capacity, and humanity could not survive an excess of wasteful conflict. We found a practical and ethical imperative for creating a peaceful, nonviolent world that offered dignified, decent lives for all. Our role became to develop innovative ways to apply our vision to create such a world.

2

Be an Applied Visionary

I t's not particularly useful for social entrepreneurs to be pure vision-aries unless they intend to start a new religion or write a philosophy textbook. Principle #2 of social entrepreneurship is "be an applied visionary." This requires being able to break down a core vision into finite, achievable pieces and then to make things happen. The goal is to produce concrete results that are consistent with that vision—or at least not incon-sistent with it.

Although social entrepreneurs may have an enlightened vision and lofty intentions, they have no choice but to move forward one step at a time. They should be what I call *salami slicers*. In other words, they need to have a knack for slicing off one attainable piece at a time. If they go for an overwhelming, unified solution—a *magic bullet*—they are likely to fail. However, if a part of their overall goal is within reach, that probably is the place for them to start.

A small victory is almost always more useful than a large failure. By scoring a success, even a modest one, social entrepreneurs can lay the groundwork for achieving their overall objectives. And their timing needs to be right. If they move too quickly or are too far ahead of the curve, they will probably be viewed as dreamers who are out of touch with reality. However, if they are too slow in reacting to an opportunity and others have already become engaged, there may be little reason for them to proceed.

I have found that being six months to a year in front of conventional wisdom is a good place to be when doing groundbreaking work.

An example of how I applied my vision in a way that managed to be ahead of where governments were—but not too far ahead—follows. I am referring to the counterterrorism project whose concluding dinner was celebrated at the Holiday Inn in Santa Monica, California, described in the prologue.

In those Cold War days, I believed the best way to stimulate the "new manner of thinking" Einstein called for was to develop initiatives that brought Soviets and Americans together to achieve shared goals. Instead of facing each other as enemies, they could stand side by side, take on common problems, and cooperate to resolve issues. This approach called for getting key players from both countries to focus on what united them rather than on what separated them. It did not require either group to give up strongly held positions or to compromise its principles. Not only could their joint action have an important impact in its own right, but we Searchers believed it could also build confidence that would lead to finding solutions to major disputes. This approach did not necessitate ignoring the many aspects of the Soviet system that Americans found abhorrent—such as human rights violations, lack of freedom, and occupation of Eastern Europe—instead it involved not letting those differences alone define the relationship.

A proponent of a similar strategy was the same Ronald Reagan who in 1983 had called the Soviet Union the "Evil Empire." Two years later Reagan was meeting with Soviet leader Mikhail Gorbachev in Geneva, and Gorbachev later told an American TV audience this story: "President Reagan suddenly said to me, 'What would you do if the United States were attacked by someone from outer space? Would you help us?' I said, 'No doubt about it.'" Although this story may sound hard to believe, it was later confirmed by former Secretary of State George Shultz, who was present in the room as the two presidents talked.

I did not agree with Reagan on most matters, and I certainly saw no possibility that there would be an attack from Mars. But I was an applied visionary who realized that Reagan's idea of bringing adversaries together around a subject of mutual concern could be useful in achieving what social psychologist Muzafer Sherif described as a "superordinate goal"—that is, a shared objective that is jointly pursued by parties in conflict.

At a Search workshop in South Africa, I mentioned this strategy to Andrew Masondo, a one-time warrior who had headed the "Spear of the

Nation," the armed wing of the African National Congress (ANC). Now that apartheid had ended, he was thinking like a peacemaker. He listened to what I described I wanted to do, and he summed up Search's approach thusly: "Understand the differences; act on the commonalities." We made his articulation into our organizational mantra.

My first attempt to operationalize this concept was a scheme to get the United States and the Soviet Union to collaborate in immunizing the world's children against childhood diseases such as measles, whooping cough, and diphtheria. In those long-ago days before vaccines were a divisive political issue, I believed that even ardent Cold Warriors would not oppose expanding their use. I reasoned that the USSR and the United States could be convinced to work together for the greater good. I assumed that saving the lives of children was an obvious commonality, but that did not prove to be the case. To my disappointment, the initiative did not achieve the intended results, but it did turn out very well on the unintended side.

As good an idea as this might have been, if a small organization like Search were the proposer, I believed we would probably be ignored. However, if I could somehow convince an actual government to invite the United States and the USSR to participate, the two countries would be more likely to say "yes." I thought Canada would make a good convener because what I was proposing seemed consistent with that country's peace building and humanitarian traditions, as exemplified by former Prime Minister Lester Pearson. Also, I had an introduction to a key Canadian ambassador, so there seemed to be a pathway to top-level approval.

I made an appointment to see the Canadian ambassador to whom I had been referred. He liked the idea and said he would propose it to the powers that be in Ottawa. Later, a well-placed Canadian diplomat told me what had happened to my proposal. The good news was that Canadian policymakers agreed to carry out a comprehensive initiative to immunize children, and they allocated a large sum of money to the project. The bad news, from my perspective, was that they eliminated the part of the proposal that called for inviting Americans and Soviets to work together in the implementation. It seemed that the Canadians did not want to do something that might displease the U.S. government. In those early days of the Reagan presidency—before Gorbachev had implemented *glasnost* and *perestroika*—the United States was not keen on positive initiatives that included the Soviet Union. My source said I should be proud because the Canadian immunization program presumably saved many lives, but I was disappointed. My goal had been to reduce the adversarial quality of the Cold War—in addition to saving the lives of children.

This was one of the first examples of a phenomenon I would witness many times in my career as an activist social entrepreneur: namely, that the unintended consequences of an initiative often ended up being as good or better than the intended ones. In this case, I would have preferred a different outcome, but I also realized that I would be wise to embrace a positive result whenever it occurred, regardless of whether it had been part of the original plan.

Like a child's windup toy truck that moves forward until it hits an obstacle and then backs off and finds another way around, I persisted in my search for a superordinate project. In 1988, I found what I was looking for, and the timing was very important, if not everything. By then, the Cold War was winding down, and the Gorbachev-led Soviet Union was losing its sinister reputation. There is an old saying that it is easier to ride a horse in the direction it is going. At this point in the Reagan-Gorbachev bromance, the two countries were already moving away from a contentious relationship, and détente was becoming a reality. The project I came up with would have been impossible a few years earlier, but now it seemed feasible. In my view, it was within the range of possible intergovernmental action, but Moscow and Washington had not yet gotten around to doing it. This left an opening for our Track 2 diplomacy.[1]

I got my chance to launch the project while I was attending a conference sponsored by the Center for Soviet-American Dialogue. This was a meeting of several hundred Americans and Soviets who were asked to brainstorm ways to improve relations between the two superpowers. The idea was for participants to develop cooperative projects. I was assigned the task of cochairing a working group on security issues, and my Soviet counterpart was Igor Beliaev, a well-known writer for a popular Soviet publication, *Literaturnaya Gazeta*. Beliaev and I, although not instant soulmates, got along well, and I convinced him that our best chance to make a difference was to identify a single issue on which effective

---

1. Track 2 diplomacy is a phrase coined by former Foreign Service Officer Joseph Montville at a 1980 meeting I attended at the Esalen Institute in Big Sur, California. It refers to unofficial, people-to-people initiatives—as opposed to Track 1, which involves official dealings between governments. Track 2 has become the universally accepted term for such activities, which Esalen's Soviet-American program pioneered in carrying out.

Soviet-American collaboration might be possible. Regional conflicts, such as those in Afghanistan and Nicaragua, seemed too well entrenched in the official agendas of the two governments for us as *citizen diplomats* to make an impact, so Beliaev and I looked for another issue on which we could productively work. We agreed that we needed to find a subject that was important—but not overly so. We decided that the prevention of terrorism would be our focus, and we signed a memorandum of understanding (MOU) to establish what we rather grandly called the U.S.-Soviet Task Force to Prevent Terrorism.

Terrorism may seem like a strange choice in today's context, but in the days before 9/11, it was not a front-burner issue. Thus it seemed more susceptible to our Track 2 approach than matters that were regularly in the headlines. Certainly, the United States had terrorism experts, but they were not at the forefront of the foreign policy field. According to Beliaev, until 1985 in the Soviet Union, the prevailing view had been that terrorism was a Western problem of concern only to capitalists. Then four Soviet officials were kidnapped in Beirut, and the Soviet government for the first time condemned an act of terrorism aimed at its citizens abroad. Subsequently, the terrorists murdered one of their hostages and raised fears in Moscow that all Soviets traveling abroad would become targets. At this point, according to rumors that widely circulated in the West but were officially denied in Moscow, KGB operatives supposedly seized an accomplice of the suspected kidnappers and castrated him. Whether or not there is any truth to this story, the three remaining hostages were soon released. Afterward, Western terrorist experts spoke enviously of this Soviet *no-nonsense* approach to counterterrorism.

In any case, terrorism did not fit comfortably within the Soviet concept of class struggle. During the Cold War, Soviets and, for that matter, Americans were inclined to look at terrorism through the prism of national liberation movements and ideological clashes. There was an oft-repeated saying that one side's freedom fighters were the other's terrorists. For Americans and Soviets alike, what seemed to matter most was the organizational affiliation of the terrorist—or freedom fighter—not the nature of the acts committed. During those years, the United States and the USSR both backed groups that used what today would be termed "terror tactics." The two countries and their allies regularly supported violent, unconventional warriors whose struggle was opposed by the other superpower. For example, in Afghanistan the United States funded and armed the mujahideen, who routinely used bombing and assassination in their fight against the communist government and the Soviet occupiers. Similarly, America supported the Contras in Nicaragua and UNITA in Angola, both of which the Soviets and their allies branded as terrorists who were violently trying to overthrow legitimate governments. The Soviets, for their part, supported the Viet Cong and the Palestine Liberation Organization, which both used tactics the U.S. government called terroristic. Despite all this history, our U.S.-Soviet Task Force took on the mission of showing that the fight against terrorism was a shared problem faced by both countries—and thus an area of possible common ground.

The task force's first meeting took place in Moscow in January 1989. It had taken eleven months for Beliaev and me to piece together the event, which was cosponsored by our two organizations, Search for Common Ground and *Literaturnaya Gazeta* (with the support of the Soviet Peace Committee). Participants included scholars, journalists, lawyers, and officials who were experts in terrorism and security issues. The original plan had been to invite only unofficial, Track 2 participants, but Beliaev put together a Soviet delegation that consisted of officials on active duty with the Ministry of Foreign Affairs, the Ministry of Internal Affairs, and several institutes inside the government's Academy of Sciences. On the American side, more than half of the dozen participants were part-time consultants to the U.S. government on terrorism-related issues. Our Track 2 gathering had become Track 1.5, and that proved to be a good thing because both Beliaev and I wanted to influence official policy. We recognized that having government officials directly involved, supposedly in their private capacity, increased the chances that our efforts would be successful.

I chose the American delegation by networking and referral. Most of the people I approached were initially skittish about participating. There were fears that their involvement might put their security clearances at risk or otherwise offend key people inside the U.S. government. My recruiting pitch was to invite potential participants to travel to Moscow to meet with their Soviet counterparts. This was an invitation to which American terror experts were inclined to say "yes" because they were curious about what they might find out. Most of them had never before gone to Moscow for professional reasons. Counterterrorism gatherings tended to be held in cities like Washington, D.C., London, and Tel Aviv, and the American experts had not, on the whole, previously considered that they might even have Soviet counterparts.

Still, the task force would never have existed if I had listened to U.S. government officials who, during the months I was putting together the project, actively tried to suppress the effort. On several occasions, officials expressed concern that I was being duped and that the Soviets would use the proceedings for propaganda purposes. In fact, just before the American delegation was scheduled to leave for Moscow, one of the participants, Colonel Augustus Richard "Dick" Norton, a tenured associate professor at West Point and a decorated combat infantryman, was summoned to the Pentagon to meet the Vice Chief of Staff of the U.S. Army, Arthur E. Brown Jr., a four-star general. Norton had never before been ordered to attend a meeting with such a high-ranking officer.

General Brown wanted to discuss the forthcoming meeting in Moscow, and he was clearly unhappy about it. As Norton later put it, the general showed "discernible discomfit." Although the general did not order him not to go, Norton concluded that as a career U.S. Army officer it would probably be prudent for him to drop out. He now believes that most other American officers would have done so. Nevertheless, he courageously held his ground, and he did not cancel. Thirty years later, Norton told me that he had been "intrigued by the possibility of success." He felt that his "academic freedom as a member of the U.S. Military Academy faculty offered intellectual license." Shortly thereafter, he resigned his commission and left the Army.

By the time Norton and the rest of the group got to Moscow, the U.S. government clearly had softened its opposition and had started to use the task force as a sounding board for new approaches. During the month preceding the first meeting, the incoming George H. W. Bush administration gave us its tacit blessing and asked for a full report. The week before the task force convened, the KGB's Deputy Director, General Vitaly Ponomarev, declared publicly:

> We realize we have to coordinate efforts to prevent terrorist acts, including hijackings of planes. . . . We are willing, if there is a need, to cooperate even with the CIA, the British intelligence service, the Israeli Mossad, and other services in the West.

A high State Department official estimated that this statement from the top of the KGB was timed to have an impact on our meeting. Within days James Baker testified at his confirmation hearing to be U.S. Secretary of

State saying, "We ought to find out whether Moscow can be helpful on [terrorism] . . . and if not, why not."

Although this high-level attention gave our group cause for optimism, the participants who headed to Moscow remained skeptical that anything useful would be accomplished. Cold War attitudes died hard, and the notion that the other superpower had something constructive to offer seemed far-fetched to many.

Both American and Soviet participants were taking risks. The Americans feared they might appear naive, or they might be walking into a Soviet trap. Soviet participants were afraid that even talking to Americans about preventing terrorism would be interpreted by their friends in the Third World as abandonment or even a hostile act.

At the event, no one's worst fears were realized, and things turned out much better than most of the participants expected. Those present were able to speak and probe without representing fixed governmental positions, which is one of the virtues of Track 2 diplomacy. At the opening session I announced that at 3:00 a.m. the next morning there would be an optional meeting at which participants could engage in polemics; that everyone was free to attend; but that I would not be coming myself. Participants laughed, and from that point on contentious statements were mostly listened to and not directly opposed. In this way, major arguments were avoided, and the atmosphere remained calm and fruitful.

One member of the U.S. delegation was Marguerite Millhauser (now Miriam Millhauser Castle), an expert not in terrorism but on conflict resolution. Search was an organization that prided itself on running meetings that produced positive results. Then and now Searchers put a high premium on the use of good processes, and meetings were often led by skilled facilitators who were able to maintain a level playing field while moving the agenda forward. At our sessions in Moscow, both Soviets and Americans accepted that our facilitator had a mandate to break deadlocks and contribute to the process of collaborative problem-solving.

Participants quickly reached an understanding that traditional ways of discussing terrorism had led nowhere and that they needed to develop a new approach for framing the issue. Both sides agreed that it was futile to try to define who specifically was a terrorist or who was a freedom fighter. Instead, they identified specific acts that, without exception, they decided constituted terrorism. These included:

- Hijacking or bombing of airplanes
- Taking of hostages
- Attacking children or internationally protected persons, including doctors, diplomats, and aid workers

Participants were unanimous that acts such as these should always be considered to be criminal, regardless of the political affiliation of the perpetrators. In other words, blowing up a civilian airplane was never to be regarded as acceptable—no matter how noble the motivating cause.

Once the participants adopted this approach, they were able to make thirty specific recommendations of tactics and techniques to prevent the forbidden acts. These involved cooperation in such areas as intelligence-sharing, joint targeting of narco-terrorists, thwarting money laundering, freeing hostages, and limiting the transfer of weapons and explosives. There was a consensus that ideological differences should not stand in the way of the two countries working together to prevent heinous activities. The idea was to separate out—or salami-slice—areas that were ripe for agreement while agreeing to disagree on the rest.

The task force largely avoided the twin pitfalls of assigning blame for past sins and making vague statements about the abstract future. Participants accepted that neither country would be likely to cease and desist all activities that the other found objectionable and labeled as terroristic. Progress would not be contingent on either government being required to change long-standing policies. Cooperation would be implemented *in addition to*—not *instead of*—existing unilateral efforts, and it would be based on the two nations recognizing that their national security interests were best served by collaborating where possible to reduce the common danger. With these conclusions, the group succeeded in reframing the core issue of terrorism, and in the process it drained gasoline from the volatile U.S.-Soviet relationship.

After the meetings ended, the recommendations were reported directly to the White House and to the Kremlin, and they attracted considerable media attention in both countries. Within two months, Foreign Minister Eduard Shevardnadze and Secretary of State James Baker agreed to put anti-terrorist cooperation on the superpower agenda, and then the two governments began working-level meetings and reached their first agreements on cooperation to prevent terrorism.

Both Soviet and American task force participants believed that their work contributed to this new collaboration, and everyone was particularly pleased during the following months when the U.S. and Soviet governments cooperated to prevent the execution of Joseph Cicippio, an American who was being held hostage in Lebanon. Indeed, one American task force member, Brian Jenkins of the Rand Corporation, told a BBC interviewer that without the efforts of the task force the Soviet-American cooperation that he believed saved Cicippio's life would not have taken place.

Even though the Moscow meeting turned out well, several participants urged that the task force should be expanded to include people with hands-on operational experience in counterterrorism, and that such people were usually found in intelligence agencies. I wholeheartedly agreed, but Beliaev was initially skeptical that high-level Soviet spooks—even former ones—could be enrolled. Without waiting for his approval, I decided to gently push his hand. I recruited former CIA director William Colby and former deputy director Ray Cline. Then I sent a telex to Moscow (telexes were a pre-internet way of communicating) telling Beliaev that Colby and Cline had agreed to come to the next meeting that was going to be held in Santa Monica. I requested that the Soviets include in their delegation retired intelligence officials of "comparable protocol rank." I must have found the right language for such an invitation because soon thereafter Beliaev telexed "yes." He wrote that he had added to the task force Feodor Sherbak and Valentin Zvezdenkov, both retired, high-level KGB generals.

Around this same time I learned that Beliaev, my Soviet counterpart, was related by marriage to Vladimir Kryuchkov, the director of the KGB. Without this connection, I do not believe the Soviets would have been willing to include participants like Sherbak and Zvezdenkov.

As appreciative as I was that the task force was now going to have both KGB and CIA participation, there was an unexpected side effect. Many of the Soviet participants decided that I must be a CIA employee, which I definitely was not. They came to this belief because in their country it probably would have been impossible to involve high-level spies—even retired ones—without personal connections to the intelligence agencies, and they projected this perspective onto the United States.

Never before had former top KGB officials come to the United States to hold friendly meetings with their American counterparts. At Search, we believed that this unprecedented development showed the importance the KGB and the Soviet government under Gorbachev placed on our meetings.

However, all didn't go seamlessly for us in California. General Sherbak's suitcase did not turn up when the Pan American Airlines plane carrying the Soviets landed in Los Angeles. In fact, his luggage was permanently lost. Soviet and American participants alike agreed that this was probably not a case of standard baggage mishandling. Everyone smelled the harassing hand of the CIA or the FBI. We Searchers made an emergency payment to Sherbak, and we took him to the Sears store in downtown Santa Monica to buy new clothes and toilet articles. He clearly was not amused by the incident, but he was very professional about it. He did not let the loss limit his participation.

Another problem was money. Our deal with the Soviets was that they would pay for their airline tickets on Aeroflot from Moscow to New York and that Search would be responsible for flying them on to Los Angeles. That seemed fair, but unfortunately Search didn't have sufficient funds available to take care of our share. So Allen Grossman, Search's board chair who was an active participant in the project, and I bridged the gap by contributing frequent flyer miles to obtain the needed tickets. Grossman and I agreed that the project was too important to be deterred by not having enough money on hand to pay all the costs.

In what was clearly a mischievous move on my part, once the Soviets arrived in California, I took them for a Sunday afternoon walk on the boardwalk along Venice Beach, which is next to Santa Monica. There they saw America at its freakiest and funkiest. Subsequently, they were taken to Disneyland where they viewed the country on a more wholesome level.

By coincidence, I flew to Los Angeles on the same plane as former CIA director William Colby, and we wound up sitting across the aisle from each other. He asked me what I thought he could contribute to the meeting. I said I hoped to see an agreement between Americans and Soviets for the exchange of intelligence to combat terrorism. He took out some scrap paper and wrote a brief description describing the mechanics of establishing such a liaison channel.

After the meeting started, the former CIA and KGB officials—plus Beliaev and me—formed what was euphemistically called the *subcommittee on information*. Colby made a presentation to the group that contained what he had previously written on the airplane, and it became the basis for the understanding that the retired Soviet and American intelligence professionals eventually reached. Specifically, they agreed that both sides needed to protect *sources and methods* but that their former services should exchange intelligence that would aid the other in preventing terrorism. The ex-KGB men made clear that future cooperation would probably result in terrorist groups targeting Soviets, but they said that the added risk was necessary to curb terrorism. The group also recommended that neither the United States nor the USSR should provide weapons to armed groups that would be useful to terrorists (e.g., surface-to-air missiles or plastic explosives).

Ray Cline, another American participant who had once been CIA deputy director and for whom I had directly worked in my earlier career in the U.S. diplomatic service, wrote an article about our meetings that was published in the *Washington Post*. He said that before attending the sessions in Santa Monica, he had only dealt with the KGB in "an essentially adversarial context." He continued:

The KGB came to the United States to assure some of those who would understand that whatever happened in the past, it really wants to exchange information with US intelligence agencies to suppress terrorists now. What they can and will deliver remains to be explored in official channels. But Gorbachev's seriousness of intent was crystal clear. Our private scholars' delegation was getting an official message.

Needless to say, the convening of top-level retired CIA and KGB officials attracted considerable attention in both the Soviet and American medias. The *Los Angeles Times* headlined that it was an "unprecedented joint effort." ABC-TV's *Nightline* devoted a whole show to the prospect of cooperation to prevent terrorism. Host Ted Koppel introduced the program by saying:

If you find it difficult to believe that the CIA and the KGB might be on the verge of cooperating with one another in the near future, your instincts are probably right. Nevertheless, high-ranking former officials from both agencies have been meeting out in California this week at a conference sponsored by the Rand Corporation and an organization called Search for Common Ground.

It seemed to me that Koppel rolled his eyes when he said the words "Search for Common Ground." In any event, this initiative not only gave us our first significant media exposure but also propelled us into the realm of popular culture, and T-shirts soon appeared for sale in Washington, D.C. that said, "Together at Last! The New KGB/CIA. Now We're Everywhere."

Participants agreed that they would take the task force's recommendations back to their governments. The retired KGB generals, Sherbak and Zvezdenkov, reported directly to KGB Director Kruyuchkov and his senior staff, and in December 1989 the KGB Politburo formally accepted the task force's recommendations on the need for intelligence-sharing with the CIA. However, when Colby and Cline took the same proposals to CIA Director William Webster, they were rebuffed on the grounds that the KGB was a secret police organization, not an intelligence agency like the CIA. Webster emphatically stated that there was no equivalence between the two secret services, that the CIA had no intention of cooperating with the KGB, and that our task force should take its recommendations to the State Department.

That is where things rested until something happened that no one had foreseen and that brought the task force's recommendations to the CIA's front burner. In August 1990, Iraq invaded Kuwait, and America's national security establishment began to prepare for what would be called the Gulf War. The U.S. government suddenly had a great need for intelligence on Iraq, and it had few assets there. It became clear that the intelligence agency with the most prior experience and best connections in Iraq was the KGB, and the CIA was now under pressure from the White House to seek its help. In October 1990, CIA Director Webster told the Associated Press that his agency and the KGB were sharing intelligence about terrorist threats and that, on several occasions, U.S. information had been "pivotal" to Soviet preventive action.

It will probably never be known to what extent our U.S.-Soviet Task Force to Prevent Terrorism was responsible for this cooperation. Nevertheless, it can be said that the possibility of such cooperation had not seriously been raised before the task force got involved, and that our recommendation for an intelligence exchange between the CIA and the KGB was eventually accepted. If the task force had not existed, probably a similar liaison channel would have been, by necessity, set up. The Gulf War certainly was a catalytic event, and our task force was unquestionably in the right place at the right time.

This project, which Beliaev and I describe in the book *Common Ground on Terrorism* (figure 2.1), turned out to be a breakthrough for me personally and for Search as an organization. The evening after the retired spooks

FIGURE 2.1 Book cover of *Common Ground on Terrorism*, published by Norton in 1991.

reached agreement in Santa Monica, I invited them to the Holiday Inn for the celebratory dinner described in the prologue. To get the conversation started, which is always difficult with covert operators who are usually reluctant to provide personal information about themselves, I asked those around the table to talk about their background. To set an example, I went first. I said that I had resigned from the State Department in protest after the United States invaded Cambodia in 1970, and that I had later written books that were critical of the CIA. KGB General Zvezdenkov responded,

"So you were a troublemaker." To his credit, Colby, my one-time adversary, responded, "I can confirm he was a troublemaker, but now we are working together for the greater good."

That was an important moment for me because it seemed to represent the completion of my previous career when my work had been defined by what I was *against*. Now, instead of being critical of the old system, I was working with former adversaries to build a new system. With no apologies for what I had previously done, my job was transformed into being *for* something—for making the world more peaceful and cooperative.

As for Search, the success of the project caused the outside world to see us as a more serious organization. The initiative greatly exceeded expectations, and *Foreign Affairs*, the establishment journal, called our efforts "pioneer work." We had previously been operating on the fringes, and this initiative helped move us into the mainstream. To get there, we had stayed true to our vision, and we had not in any way compromised our values. It helped hugely that the world was moving away from the belief that the fundamental issue of international relations was the clash between capitalism and communism. History was definitely headed in the direction we desired.

Although the Cold War was coming to an end, we recognized that there was no shortage of other conflicts where we could take a similar approach. In the years that followed, we turned our attention away from the Soviet Union and Russia and focused on the Middle East, Africa, and the Balkans. We became global Search.

3

On s'engage, et puis on voit

Principle 3 of social entrepreneurship is *"on s'engage, et puis on voit."* A nonliteral translation from the original French is "one becomes engaged in an activity, and then one sees new possibilities."

Napoleon Bonaparte, a soldier by profession, first uttered these words. Engaging the enemy and then seeing the opportunities reflected his military perspective. He understood that the best way to discern the shape of the defenses of the troops he faced was to attack and then base subsequent moves on the enemy's reaction. As a peace-loving civilian, I only applied this Napoleonic principle metaphorically. I didn't go around beating up opponents to see how they defended themselves.

The lesson for social entrepreneurs—and business entrepreneurs, for that matter—is that once engaged in an activity they will see openings that were not visible at the start. In this way, they will discover paths forward that they had not known existed. Out of their engagement can come the building blocks for what comes next—and next and next.

This way of operating—*on s'engage, et puis on voit*—became a key part of how I functioned in building Search. I found it almost impossible to plan ahead more than a few moves—both when starting a new project and when bringing an existing one to fruition. Rather, by being engaged, unforeseen prospects often emerged from what had come before. Sticking slavishly to a predetermined plan did not usually work,

30

and excessive planning was often a barrier to moving forward. As boxing champion Mike Tyson once said, "Everyone has a plan until they've been punched in the mouth." The Soviets learned this the hard way with their five-year plans.

As a general rule, successful entrepreneurs need to be able to make midcourse corrections that grow out of their prior engagement. But accepting the need for continuing adjustments is not easy for people who prize regularity and predictability. Nor is it easy for entrenched bureaucrats who want to be told exactly what the plan is. If budding social entrepreneurs find it distressing not to know what the outcome will be, and if they cannot deal well with the unexpected, they should probably make a different career choice. Successful social entrepreneurship almost always requires a high tolerance for ambiguity. Practitioners need to be comfortable with *not knowing*. It usually helps considerably if they have confidence that they are likely to wind up in a good place no matter what happens.

On s'engage, et puis on voit worked well for me on the personal as well as on the professional level. I cite the case of my own love life. When I founded Search in 1982, I had no expectation of ever finding a wife with whom I would work closely. During Search's first eleven years, I was a divorced bachelor, and my private life was mostly disconnected from my job. In 1993, I traveled to South Africa to produce a television series titled *South Africa's Search for Common Ground*. On my fourth night in Cape Town, I went out for a few beers with my coproducer, a lovely Afrikaner guy named Hannes Siebert. He asked if I were married, and I answered that I was divorced. Then I said something I had never said before: "But I'm looking."

He replied, "What are you looking for?"

I answered, "A tall, beautiful mediator."

He said, "I know one."

The next day Siebert introduced me to Susan Collin (figure 3.1). She was working as a facilitator and conflict resolver in South Africa's transition from apartheid to democracy. I was smitten, and so, apparently, was she. Within twenty-six hours, we both understood that this was the real thing. After two days, Susan informed me that she and I were destined not only to be a couple but also to work together. Initially, the idea freaked me out, and it took several hours for me to internalize her declaration that the two of us would be partners both personally and professionally. Not only was I engaged, but soon we became engaged.

FIGURE 3.1 The former Susan Collin and John Marks when we met in South Africa.

Nine months after we met Susan moved to Washington, D.C., and we were married. She became Susan Collin Marks, and she joined me as Senior Vice President of Search. I would have preferred for us to be copresidents, but Search's board of directors did not approve.

Although we shared similar values and beliefs, we brought different perspectives to what became our combined work. She had a more heart-centered approach than I did, but she also contributed extraordinary intellectual and problem-solving skills. From her work in the South African peace process, she had considerable on the ground experience. She was used to working in the middle of parties in violent conflict. In fact, she had even been shot in the leg with a rubber bullet while trying to mediate between White policemen and angry Black demonstrators. I tended to operate mostly from my head, and my specialty was in putting together new projects. The qualities we brought to our work were complementary, and our relationship seemed greater than the sum of its parts. In addition, working together provided us with a constant stream of things to talk about.

Before 1994 when Susan joined me in Washington, D.C., Search's budget had been mostly stagnant. After Susan came on board, the organization grew over the next two decades at a rate of about 20 percent per year. In my view, that was not a coincidence; it was a result of our joint leadership. Harvard Business School does not teach that organizational growth depends on marrying well, but that certainly proved to be true in our case.

Susan and I came together at a time when the Cold War was winding down, and there clearly was less space for Track 2 activities in the U.S.-Soviet domain. A prime example of *on s'engage, et puis on voit* resulted in what became Search's next big thing. Here is what happened.

From their involvement with the terrorism project, Dick Norton and Salim Nasr saw a new possibility. Norton was the U.S. Army colonel a four-star general had cautioned not to travel to Moscow with the U.S.-Soviet Task Force to Prevent Terrorism. Nasr was a Lebanese professor who was then teaching at Georgetown University. The two men came up with a very interesting idea. They wanted to stop the bloody civil war in Lebanon, and they suggested that Search set up a U.S.-Soviet Task Force on Lebanon structured along the lines of what we had developed for terrorism. Both superpowers had allies who were deeply involved in the Lebanese conflict, and they surmised that a collaborative effort by Moscow and Washington could play a key role in ending the fighting. This was during the Gorbachev years when the USSR and the United States were already cooperating in several other places. Why not in Lebanon where cooperation might save lives?

I loved the idea. The fact that I had not been the one to think of it made no difference. It was clear to me that a social entrepreneur needs to be open to proposals from others—and ready to act on them if and when the moment seems right.

The prospect of a U.S.-Soviet Task Force on Lebanon did not emerge through a carefully constructed planning process. Rather, it grew organically out of a previous project, and it was a feasible follow-on. If Norton and Nasr had not been engaged, they would not have seen the possibility of taking a similar approach in Lebanon; nor would I have. I decided that was too good an opportunity to pass up, and I made a quick trip to Moscow to find out if my interest could be matched on the Soviet side. As had been the case with the Task Force to Prevent Terrorism, I knew that a successful initiative would require the right Soviet partner. In Moscow I talked with a number of people about whether the project was achievable, and if so, what would be the best organization with which to work. In the end, I joined forces with the Middle East department of the Institute of World Economy and International Relations of the Soviet Academy of Sciences. This institute, which had been headed by Yevgeni Primakov who would subsequently become Russia's prime minister, agreed to cosponsor the task force and to choose ten prominent Soviets to be part of it. We agreed that participants should be people who were nominally unofficial but who had access to policymakers.

Next, I went back to Washington, D.C. and put together a comparable American team of ten Middle East specialists. In November 1990, I returned to Moscow with the Americans. At the first session, something happened that changed the nature of the project. The group had begun to engage when William Quandt, former director of Middle East Affairs of the U.S. National Security Council, stated convincingly that the idea of the United States and the USSR working together in Lebanon would not be effective— not because the two countries could not cooperate but because the Lebanese civil war was inextricably tied to other conflicts in the Middle East. He noted that peace in Lebanon required a regional approach. He pointed out that the parties in Lebanon's civil war had sponsors both inside and outside the region. After considerable discussion, participants agreed that the project should take on a wider Middle East approach and that its the name should be changed to the U.S.-Soviet Task Force on the Middle East and Lebanon. There was a shared feeling that it was time to explore new approaches. In the end, the group recommended that the USSR and the United States should convene under UN auspices an ongoing Track 1 process for the Middle East similar to the 1975 Helsinki Conference on Security and Cooperation in Europe (CSCE, now OSCE), which provided a framework for reducing East-West tensions.

After returning to the United States, I briefed Allen Grossman, my board chair, on what had happened in Moscow. I told him about our plan for Search to become an advocate for an official, intergovernmental,

CSCE-type process. However, he misunderstood what I was proposing. He thought I was saying that we at Search would convene an unofficial Track 2 process for regional cooperation in the Middle East. My first impulse was to correct him, but I quickly realized that, at least from Search's perspective, the premise at the heart of his misunderstanding—to work unofficially—would be a better approach than what the task force had proposed in Moscow. Lobbying the superpowers to establish an official CSCE-type process was not in itself a bad idea, but it was outside Search's skill set; whereas holding unofficial Track 2 meetings within a CSCE-like regional framework would be consistent with our strongest suit. Thus I decided to make a change in strategy. Instead of lobbying governments to set up an official Track 1 structure, we Searchers would ourselves launch a shadow CSCE process on an unofficial Track 2 level.

Even though this particular change worked out well, readers should not think that moving ahead on the basis of a misunderstanding is necessarily a key part of social entrepreneurship. The lesson here is that social entrepreneurs need to be prepared to take advantage of new opportunities, no matter how they arise. And if social entrepreneurs are not deeply engaged, they are likely to miss these chances.

My colleagues and I were able to frame what we had in mind by saying it would be like CSCE—but for the Middle East. Our target audience in the foreign policy and funding communities easily understood this metaphor.

Although the CSCE process had worked very well in Europe, we knew that our unofficial structure would have to reflect both the realities of the Middle East and our organizational limitations. Our idea was to create a core group that brought together a wide variety of people from across the region: retired generals, human rights activists, business executives, editors, and conflict resolution experts. Not only would these people engage in dialogue, but they would also work together on joint action projects. In addition, we hoped to chronicle and promote regional cooperation by publishing a quarterly newsletter. We knew that CSCE had existed for about fifteen years before it had become effective in improving East-West relations. We anticipated our process might take at least that long and would involve numerous meetings.

Once we had decided on the project's basic approach, the next step was to find funding. That was not easy to do with an initiative unlike anything that had ever been tried in the Middle East. However, in the same way that an unexpected event—the build-up to the Gulf War—had contributed to the success of our U.S.-Soviet Task Force to Prevent Terrorism, our Middle East work received a boost from another event we had not anticipated—the outbreak of the Gulf War itself. We were once again ahead of the curve because our project's core elements had been developed before the war had even begun. As much as my colleagues and I detested war and the resulting loss of life, the Gulf War turned out to be a boon for us: it validated the idea that the region was in need of a comprehensive, CSCE-type process. Although we did not fully understand this at the time, our timing was impeccable.

Events played out as follows. Our Moscow meeting on Lebanon and the Middle East took place in November 1990, and the Gulf War began about six weeks later in January 1991. By the end of February the fighting had ended, and my colleagues and I had already written most of our proposal. However, nothing was yet in concrete, and we were agile enough to make revisions that reflected the evolving state of the region. By this point in our organizational life, we had learned how important it was to use donors' favorite buzz words and to frame proposals in language that spoke directly to their needs and preferences—while still maintaining the integrity of the project. Instead of emphasizing that our aim was to promote regional cooperation, which it continued to be, we stressed that this was an effort to help restore peace in the region, which it also was.

Because the project was now regional in nature, concentrating on Lebanon seemed to make little sense, so we changed the proposal to eliminate our focus on that country. Also, with the Cold War waning and Soviet influence in the Middle East lessening, a U.S.-Soviet approach, which had previously seemed crucial, no longer felt necessary. So we dropped the Soviet involvement and renamed the project the Initiative for Peace and Cooperation in the Middle East. Our operating strategy became to complement, supplement, and, on occasion, anticipate official negotiations in the region.

These changes made the proposal more yesable, and we received our first ever six-figure grants from the John D. and Catherine T. MacArthur Foundation, the Ford Foundation, and the W. Alton Jones Foundation. These grants enabled us to begin an innovative new project, and they also improved our chances of receiving heftier contributions from other donors. Most funders are reluctant to make larger donations than those the organization has already received. In our case, bigger sums started to flow in once we had cracked the six-figure barrier.

With the money in hand to launch the project, we set about choosing twenty-five Middle Easterners to be members of the Initiative's Core

Working Group. We were looking for influential thinkers who were also action-oriented. These Arabs, Israelis, Iranians, and Turks were to be at the heart of our process. We planned to establish a forum in which Middle Easterners would meet, not as adversaries but as colleagues. Participants would share superordinate goals and work together to resolve common problems.

In addition, we recognized that in the Middle East, as in other regions, Track 2 work with influential participants often required at least the tacit approval of top level Track 1 officials. Armed with introductions from our various contacts, the executive director of the Initiative, retired Ambassador Peter Constable, and I traveled to the region to hold meetings with leaders of the Egyptian, Israeli, and Jordanian governments. Another colleague connected with top officials of the Palestine Liberation Organization (PLO). The basic question we asked of the people with whom we met was not how to make peace in the region but what well-placed people would they recommend for participation in confidential, unofficial talks?

In the abstract, the Initiative and its Core Working Group seemed like a great idea. As we began, however, we did not know if it would actually work. Would high-level, unofficial, Middle Easterners agree to get involved—and stay involved for long periods of time? And, if so, would they be able to accomplish anything?

We got our initial answer in Rome in September 1991 at the first Core Working Group meeting, when participants met for three days at the airport Holiday Inn. As much as I would have preferred a hotel with more ambiance, we wanted to avoid calling attention to what we were doing, and a grand hotel in the center of Rome would have been considerably less private—not to mention more expensive. In addition, we were concerned about security, as was the Italian government with which we were in close contact. After all, in those days before official Middle Eastern talks had begun in Madrid, there were people in the world—and there still are—who did not think Arabs, Israelis, Iranians, and Turks should be consorting with each other and who might have reacted violently if they knew what we were doing. As a result, Italian authorities provided us with security in the form of a Carabinieri, who wielded a submachine gun, wore striped pants and a plumed hat, and guarded the door of our meeting room. I am not sure that we needed this protection, but it was better to be safe than sorry—and his armed presence did add a certain seriousness to the gathering.

Inside the meeting room, the tone was set early when an Arab participant—almost reflexively—began to criticize a right-wing Israeli general who was sitting near him. As the tension mounted, a Lebanese participant who had fought with the PLO against Israeli forces walked across the room, put his arm around the Israeli general whom he might have once faced in battle, and declared, "He is my friend." At that point, the group seemed to let out a collective sigh of relief, and the atmosphere shifted.

We knew that we wanted to avoid the *win-lose*, polemical approach that was so common in the Middle East—and in so many places. We realized that sessions needed to be interesting and productive; otherwise participants would not make the significant commitment of time that we felt would be necessary. We hoped our meetings would provide a prototype for future regional cooperation, and we understood full well that the process we employed to run these meetings was likely to be as important as the substance of what was discussed.

As we had done with the terrorism project, we brought in a professional facilitator. We understood that using a facilitator—as opposed to having a senior person act as the chair and call on people who raise their hands—was not usually part of international gatherings. Nevertheless, we decided to utilize a culturally sensitive facilitator both to moderate the proceedings and to help structure the overall process. We enlisted Marc Sarkady, a corporate consultant in the organizational development field. To his credit, he agreed to work with us on a *pro bono* basis.

At the Rome meeting, participants were initially mystified by Sarkady's role. One participant even quipped that he thought a facilitator was a kind of enema. Nonetheless, most of the participants quickly came to like the process, and Sarkady became a rallying point for group cohesiveness. Participants tended to see him as the guardian of a level playing field, particularly between Palestinians and Israelis. When there was a breakdown in the discussion, or when something was not understood, or even when someone's body language indicated unhappiness, Sarkady spent considerable time setting things right. He explained concepts such as active listening, and participants started paying attention with an intensity that was very different from the empty stares that were so often the norm at meetings of Middle Easterners.

One participant, a well-known Egyptian human rights activist, later related how he briefed his wife and kids on the Rome meeting after he came home. Among other things he described *active listening*, which to him was a new and exciting concept. One of his teenage sons took it all in and then asked, "Dad, does that mean that now you have to listen to us?"

The meetings began with hard-headed, policy-oriented discussions. However, friendships quickly formed across national lines, and people found that they genuinely liked each other. Participants arrived on time and asked for longer sessions. There was remarkable frankness, a willingness to work through obstacles, a determination to try out new ideas, and a commitment to results. As stereotypes were broken down, many participants felt they were part of something historic. They agreed on a set of operating principles and formed a series of working groups to deal with pressing issues.

On the substantive level, there were unique aspects to the meetings. First, we included right-wing Israelis. Most previous meetings of Arabs and Israelis had involved only dovish Israelis who reflected a limited perspective. Most of the Arabs had never met an Israeli hawk. Second, Saudis and Gulf Arabs sat together with Israelis (and talked amiably in the corridors and over meals). Although this has since become relatively commonplace, at the time it was revolutionary.

There were some wonderful moments, such as when Israelis and Gulf Arabs discovered that they shared common ground on at least one point: How to make sure that the American government kept its promises. Or when Arab and Israeli human rights campaigners decided in a breakout session to launch a regional campaign to prevent torture and to protect activists like themselves. Previously, the Core Working Group as a whole had decided that all new activities required the approval—or at least not the disapproval—of all the participants. And in the face of this announcement about human rights, there were two dissenters: both were former generals, one Egyptian and the other Israeli. They made exactly the same argument. They wanted everyone to understand that of course they opposed human rights abuses, but they felt that if the Initiative got deeply involved with such issues, the region's governments would oppose all of its activities. Then a Kuwaiti who had survived torture by his Iraqi captors declared with passion that if the Initiative could not take a stand against torture he was not interested in being involved. He was supported by an Israeli human rights activist. In the end, the two generals relented. They said that they did not want their objections to jeopardize the initiative as a whole and, particularly, their involvement in the Security Working Group. This was the first time participants had ever seen Israelis and Arabs arguing on both sides of an issue—which was a breakthrough in its own terms.

At the end of the Rome gathering, several attendees stated that they had never before attended a meeting at which so much was accomplished, and they requested that future sessions include training in facilitation. We said we would provide this for participants who agreed to come early.

During the next dozen years, we held scores of additional meetings, workshops, trainings, and other gatherings. Participants wrote papers, articles, and books together. They sponsored regional campaigns, appeared together on the BBC, attacked stereotypes, went on wilderness trips, and generally achieved a remarkable set of accomplishments.

One of my favorite memories that embodies the initiative's overall spirit occurred in Amman, Jordan. After a meeting of the Security Working Group, participants piled into taxis to go to dinner at a restaurant across town. By chance, I found myself in a cab with three others: Mohammad Mahallati, an Iranian; Ze'ev Schiff, an Israeli; and Ismat Kittani, an Iraqi. I was in the back seat chatting away in English with my Iranian and Israeli friends, and Kittani was in the front talking to the driver in Arabic. As Kittani later recounted, the driver asked him who we were and what we were doing in Amman. Kittani replied that the three people in the back were Mahallati, the former Iranian ambassador to the United Nations; Schiff, the dean of Israeli journalists; and me, an American who headed an NGO. Kittani added that he was an Iraqi who had been president of the UN General Assembly. The driver was incredulous. "And all this is happening in my cab!" he exclaimed.

To my mind, this taxi provided a model for exactly what my colleagues and I wanted to see across the Middle East. Our vision was to expand what was happening in that taxi to the region as a whole. Unfortunately, this vision has not yet been realized—and it is not even close today. Still, the Initiative had some extraordinary accomplishments.

- In 1993–94, before official peace talks had begun between Jordan and Israel, we sponsored back-channel meetings between former generals from both countries. Together they worked out a series of unofficial understandings that needed to be dealt with in future official negotiations between Israel and Jordan. After each of their meetings, the results were quickly passed on to the prime minister of Israel and the king of Jordan. These unofficial formulations demonstrated that there could be agreements consistent with the mutual interests of both countries, and many of their specific ideas became part of the eventual Israeli-Jordanian peace treaty that was signed in October 1994. We were about six months ahead of the official negotiations, which proved to be about right.

- For eighteen months during 1993 and 1994, we sponsored unofficial talks between Israelis and Syrians on security issues involving the Golan Heights. These talks laid the groundwork for official Syrian-Israeli negotiations. However, we were forced to stop after the existence of the meetings was leaked to the press in Israel, and the Syrian government, which had been kept in the loop from the beginning, denied any knowledge of the talks. This Syrian reaction was reminiscent of the scene in the classic movie *Casablanca* when the Claude Rains character says he is "shocked, shocked" to hear that gambling is going on.
- In 2002, we established the Middle East Consortium for Infectious Disease Surveillance (MECIDS) to bring together public health officials and academics from Israel, Jordan, and Palestine. With the goal of promoting cooperation to reduce the threat from contagious diseases, the project operated from the premises that germs do not stop at checkpoints; that cross-border detection, reporting, and data collection are crucial; and that infectious disease surveillance is virtually identical to biological warfare surveillance. (When ten people simultaneously develop flu symptoms, their governments must determine if this was a natural occurrence, or if the germs were manufactured in a laboratory.) We have managed to keep MECIDS operating for more than twenty years—from the time of avian flu through COVID-19—largely because it has stuck to professional issues and stayed out of politics.
- We regularly convened the Middle East's top editors and broadcast executives. The idea was to encourage reporting that did not inflame conflict; that reduced stereotyping; and that humanized the other. As a result, Israeli and Arab media professionals were often able to work collaboratively and exchange information in moments of crisis.
- We started the Common Ground News Service, which published articles from 2005 to 2013 on key issues affecting Muslim-Western relations. Its articles were reprinted roughly 40,000 times in newspapers and websites in the region and around the world.
- Under the chairmanship of former World Bank head and U.S. Secretary of Defense Robert McNamara, we convened two gatherings of Arab, Israeli, and Turkish business leaders. Again, we were ahead of the curve because soon thereafter the U.S. government began holding similar meetings as part of its Middle East peace process. When that happened, we suspended our meetings because we chose to work only in areas in which we did not duplicate the efforts of others.

On September 11, 2001, al-Qaeda terrorists hijacked four airliners, two of which they crashed into the twin towers of New York City's World Trade Center, killing nearly three thousand people. Osama bin Laden, al-Qaeda's leader, held the United States responsible for its years of backing Israel against the Palestinians, and he said this attack was revenge for that and for U.S. actions against Muslims in the Middle East and beyond.

In the aftermath of 9/11, my wife Susan and I concluded that the struggle between Israelis and Palestinians was the Middle East's—and the world's—core conflict, even if many more people were being killed in fighting in other places. She and I decided to de-emphasize our regional work and to focus on the Israeli-Palestinian conflict. As professional peace builders, we felt a responsibility to be engaged directly in trying to lessen the conflict. So in the midst of the second intifada when Palestine and Israel were wracked by violence, Susan and I decided to move to Jerusalem for two years.

We left management at Search's Washington, D.C. headquarters to our chief operating officer, Shamil Idriss, who a dozen years later would be my successor as CEO of Search. Due to the seven-hour time difference, we found that we could do a full day's work in Jerusalem and still put in considerable time—albeit remotely—in Washington, D.C. We moved into a lovely house, the former Turkish consulate, located seventy meters from the line that divided East and West Jerusalem. As common grounders, we would have liked to have shown our evenhandedness by living on the actual dividing line, but that would have put us in the middle of a highway. We bought produce in Palestinian East Jerusalem, where it was fresher, and we frequented supermarkets in the Israeli part of the city that were better stocked with packaged goods. There were no movie theaters on the Palestinian side, but we frequented a video store there. On weekends, we often went to the cinema at a West Jerusalem mall where young Israeli women from the settlements made fashion statements with miniskirts and M16 rifles. In a city largely segregated by ethnicity, we were among the few people who traveled back and forth freely, and we experienced the joy and pain of both sides. Indeed, we came to agree with the late Faisal Husseini, who said that Jerusalem would be either the "rising sun" or the "black hole" of the Middle East. Our work in Jerusalem was to create an environment in which the "rising sun" could emerge and shine brightly.

While we were in Jerusalem (figure 3.2), I spent most of my time writing and producing a four-part documentary TV series titled *The Shape of*

FIGURE 3.2 John Marks and Susan Collin Marks after a day's filming in southern Israel.

the Future, which focused on how to resolve the Israeli-Palestinian conflict. The idea was to show that there could be workable solutions that
were acceptable to most people on both sides. The series was made almost
totally in Arabic and Hebrew, neither of which I spoke. I used simultane-
ous translation for the interviews, which meant I was usually about seven
seconds late in sharing emotion with my subjects. Still I was in hog heaven,
and I reveled in the creative process. For me, personally, making this series
was probably the single most stimulating project on which I worked during
my thirty-two years at Search.

Two incidents stood out during my discovery process. The first came
when I was interviewing an old Palestinian man in a refugee camp outside
Jerusalem. He had been born in a village inside what is now Israel and had
been forced to leave in 1948 during the armed struggle that the Israelis call

the "War of Independence" and the Palestinians refer to as the "Nakba" (which means "disaster" in Arabic). I asked the man, who still clung to a key to his old house, whether he wanted to go back to the village he originally came from, and he vehemently answered "yes." Then I asked him if he would be willing to stay in Palestine if he were to receive a large amount of money as compensation for what he had lost, and he said "no." Next I asked if he would give up his right of return if Palestinian leader Yasser Arafat told him not to go back, and he again answered "no." Suddenly he turned the tables on me and posed a question: "Where were you born?" I replied, "New Jersey." He asked, "Could anything make you give up New Jersey?" I chuckled and said that I already had given up New Jersey and moved to Washington, D.C.

As the days passed, I realized that this exchange was certainly not at all humorous for the old man. For a Palestinian, the place where he was born—the stones, the olive trees—was sacred. To me—and also to most Americans and Israelis—the country as a whole was much more important than the specific place from which I came. I realized that this was a fundamental difference between Israelis and Palestinians that fueled the conflict: many Israelis believed that the very strong Palestinian longing to return to their native villages reflected an insatiable desire to drive the Jewish population into the sea. With more understanding of and empathy for Palestinian aspirations, I thought perhaps ways could be found to lessen some of the pain and to help discover solutions for the issues that divided these two peoples.

The second incident occurred when I went to interview a Jewish couple in Jerusalem on a Thursday night. This was the evening before the Jewish sabbath started. For many young Israelis who usually had the next day off, it was a time to party. While I was waiting for my interview subjects in their living room, their son entered and we started to talk. He was a soldier on active duty whose main task was protecting Jewish settlers in Hebron on the West Bank. He had been given leave for shabbat, and he was dressed in fancy clothes for a night on the town. In a nonprovocative way, I asked him how he liked his duty in Hebron, and he blurted out, "I am ashamed of some of the things I have seen and done."

I did not follow up because I had come to interview the parents, not the son. After a few minutes, they came into the room, and the son said goodnight and went off to a club. After he left, I told the father what I had heard from his son, and I asked for his reaction. The father replied that the young man had not meant what he said. "He's a good boy, and he wouldn't do bad things," stated the father.

To me, this was an extraordinary example of denial—denying what his own son had said only minutes before. During our two years in Jerusalem, I found that this type of denial was typical of how many, if not most, Israelis viewed their occupation of Palestine.

In 2005, the four *Shape of the Future* documentary programs I wrote and produced were broadcast on the same nights on Israeli, Palestinian, and Abu Dhabi TV. Such a cross-border simulcast had never happened before, and I was pleased with the final product, which is still available on Amazon.com two decades later. As former President Jimmy Carter said:

> This documentary series examines the fears and aspirations of Israelis and Palestinians in an even-handed way. It shows how a negotiated agreement could address those fears and aspirations without threatening the national existence of either side. Israel and Egypt were able to accomplish this task at Camp David more than 25 years ago, and this series supports the belief that Israelis and Palestinians can do the same.

After two years in Jerusalem, Susan and I went home to Washington, D.C., and we were succeeded as program directors in Jerusalem by former assistant secretary of state Robert Pelletreau and his wife Pamela. They were followed by John Bell, a former Canadian diplomat. All of these directors (including us) were expatriates from outside the region, and by choosing them we avoided showing a preference for either Palestinians or Israelis. However, in 2010 we made a big leap and named an Israeli, Sharon Rosen, and a Palestinian, Suheir Rasul, to be codirectors (figure 3.3). For the next ten years, they were partners and friends—two mothers working together for peace between their two peoples. Rosen came originally from the UK; Rasul was born in the USA. They had both returned to the Holy Land, which they considered to be their homeland, and they completely supported the right of the other to be there. For me, their relationship demonstrated what was possible—but certainly has never been achieved—between their two peoples. If only this kind of connection could be extended across the entire region!

Having been engaged in the Middle East for more than thirty years, I have seen—and acted upon—all sorts of possibilities. Although most of our projects were successful on their own terms, what we did was obviously

FIGURE 3.3 Codirectors Suheir Rasul (left) and Sharon Rosen (right) outside Search's office in Jerusalem in 2010.

not sufficient to achieve our overarching vision of regional peace. The reality is that the Middle East is further away from peace today than it was three decades ago when our involvement started. The question arises: Was it worth the effort?

I answer with an emphatic "yes." Perhaps things would be worse if we had not been involved. We will never know. Our efforts helped maintain threads of connection between Israelis, Arabs, and Iranians. We were promoting the idea that there is a better way to resolve conflicts than the violent *win-lose* and *lose-lose* approaches that have prevailed for so long in the region. We and many others with whom we shared values provided a framework for an eventual end to the conflict—and all conflicts do end at some point. Perhaps our greatest contribution was to help keep hope alive.

4

Keep Showing Up

It has been said that 80 percent of success is showing up. Principle #4 of social entrepreneurship is "keep showing up." It simply does not work to dabble in a project—or to parachute into a conflict—and then to pull out shortly thereafter without leaving behind a replacement or a whole team. In 1996, Search launched an initiative to try to improve U.S. relations with Iran, and that effort continued for twenty-five years. This project is a prime example of the operational benefits of continuing to show up.

Social entrepreneurs should be willing to make long-term commitments to all of their projects, but I found that showing up was particularly important in working with Iranians who tend to look at the world in terms of centuries and millennia. Even after Search became a multilayered organization with hundreds of employees, I stayed personally involved in our Iran work. I knew full well that management experts would advise the president of an organization of our size and complexity not to function as the desk officer for an individual project, and I understood the importance of delegating. However, by working in a direct way on the Iran project, I avoided being overwhelmed by the administrative demands of my job. Moreover, Ambassador Bill Miller, my partner in carrying out Search's effort to improve U.S.-Iranian relations, was one of my oldest and most treasured friends. I absolutely loved being able to shut my office door, put aside questions of finance and logistics, and conspire with Miller about how to move our Iran project forward. Indeed, I would counsel all social entrepreneurs that they will be more effective leaders if they retain some hands-on working-level functions.

Our work with Iran emerged directly from our sponsorship of the Initiative for Peace and Cooperation in the Middle East. Mohammad Jafar "Amir" Mahallati, the former Iranian ambassador to the UN, was a member of that project's Core Working Group. Previously, Mahallati had played a key role in negotiating an end to the Iran-Iraq War. The talks he had helped start eventually were successful, but he began the peace process before Iran's leaders were ready for meaningful negotiations. As a result, he had been removed from his UN post, which effectively ended his diplomatic career.

By 1994, Mahallati had become a regular participant in our Middle Eastern meetings, and he was impressed by the process we employed. He described his reaction this way: "For the first time, I experienced a kind of atmosphere—a kind of spirit—in a conference, in a gathering, which permits people to open themselves up without reservation and speak out of their hearts."

At one of our sessions in Marrakesh, Mahallati took me aside and suggested that Search sponsor Track 2 sessions between Iranians and Americans that were similar to what we were doing with our Middle Eastern project. He thought such meetings might cut through the mistrust that pervaded the U.S.-Iranian relationship and bring the two countries closer together. I was initially horrified by this idea. The Iran hostage crisis remained fresh in my mind, and I must confess that I still held a stereotypical view of Iranians. I knew that Mahallati's father was the Grand Ayatollah of Shiraz. Probably, like many Americans, deep down I thought all ayatollahs were religious fanatics who exhorted their followers to shout "death to America." But when I met Mahallati's dad, an actual ayatollah, my stereotype melted away. He turned out to be a wonderfully wise man with an impish smile and a lovely personality. In my view, he embodied everything a man of God should be.

Mahallati and I gradually built up enough trust to become real friends. A year after he made his proposal, I agreed to be his American partner in setting up Track 2 meetings. At the same time, I kept in mind Ronald Reagan's old adage: "Trust but verify." And I must say that since that time more than a quarter century ago when Mahallati and I agreed to work together, I never have had reason to mistrust him.

Mahallati did not have an organization behind him, but he became Search's partner and recruited the Iranian participants for our working group. They included professors and a Foreign Ministry official supposedly acting in his private capacity. We were pleased to have a Track 1 man involved in what we had foreseen would be a Track 2 process. His presence meant that at least some parts of the Iranian government—albeit relatively moderate ones—were probably going to pay attention and that the results of our meetings were likely to reach into official circles.

At Search we created a planning team that included me, my wife Susan, and William Kirby, a former U.S. deputy assistant secretary of state who was then heading our Middle East program. We were particularly interested in including Americans who had connections to current policymakers, and we enrolled in our effort a distinguished group that included a former assistant secretary of state, former National Security Council officials, a conservative think tanker, a professor, and retired ambassadors—one of whom, Bruce Laingen, had been the senior American diplomat held hostage after the 1979 seizure of the U.S. Embassy in Tehran.

Nevertheless, a well-known retired U.S. ambassador refused to participate and warned that we were putting Search at risk by meeting with Iranians. He said that such a project could result in our losing access to U.S. government funds and that, in any case, the time was not right for what we were trying to do. I noted—although I did not say this to the ambassador—that the time never seemed to be right to try to improve relations with Iran. In any case, we decided that the importance of our cause justified the risks involved in moving ahead. We felt we had an opening that should be pursued.

Planning was complicated. We had to figure out where to hold the meetings and how to pay for them. We needed to find a location where participants would feel safe to talk freely. We understood that the process probably required some level of government involvement because Iranian participants would require visas to enter most countries, and only a cooperative government could guarantee that the necessary entry permits would be issued. That ruled out holding the sessions in the United States or in Iran—neither of which was likely to support what we had in mind.

Sweden, which then had a long history of neutrality, seemed like an excellent choice. Its Foreign Ministry was already financing another Search program on regional Middle Eastern security, so we had an existing relationship in place along with a good track record. I approached a high official of the Swedish Foreign Ministry and asked for funding, visa support, and an isolated site where participants could meet and not be disturbed. After checking at the highest level, he responded that his ministry would back us—but only if the U.S. government did not object. He confided that his minister wanted to make sure there would be no damage to the country's relationship with the United States if Sweden hosted our process. The Swedes feared that our meetings might create a rift like the one that had developed during the Vietnam War when Prime Minister Olaf Palme strongly opposed U.S. policy and further alienated American officials by appearing in a widely viewed film, *I am Curious (Yellow)*, which was perceived as both antiwar and pornographic.

We recognized that the Clinton administration would be unlikely to go on the record to communicate officially that it approved our meetings, so we asked a high State Department official if he would be willing to telephone his Swedish counterpart and informally provide a green light. We never knew if this official cleared the idea with any of his colleagues, but he did make the call and told the Swedes that the U.S. government would have no objection if we went ahead. That did the trick, and the Swedes came on board.

To make it easier to justify the funding to its parliamentary watchdogs, the Swedish Foreign Ministry stipulated that the grant would need to be given to a Swedish institute that then would pass the money on to us. We had no problem with this arrangement, and we quickly formed a working partnership with the Life & Peace Institute of Uppsala, Sweden. As for a place to meet, a Swedish official recommended an isolated country inn in Sjövillan, a hamlet not far from the Stockholm airport. Not only did the inn provide a beautiful setting on the edge of a lake, but we also had the whole place to ourselves, which was important in maintaining the confidentiality of our sessions. The Sjövillan innkeeper turned into the godmother of our talks, and she took impeccable care of us.

Our Iranian participants were particularly insistent that the existence of the meetings should be kept secret. They knew that just talking to Americans, if discovered by the wrong people, could put them in physical danger. Thus, from the beginning, our participants needed to have faith in the good intentions of the others.

Despite our desire to work confidentially, we knew U.S. intelligence agencies would be likely to find out that we were meeting with Iranians, so we felt it would be wise to informally brief key people in the State Department and the White House. None of our interlocutors inside the U.S. government told us not to hold the meetings. In fact, almost everyone to whom we talked asked to be kept informed.

We held the first meeting in May 1996, and we were able to read a message to participants from President Bill Clinton. Although the message had no real substance, except to wish the participants well, it sent a signal to the Iranians that the White House was aware of what was happening and that the American participants were serious about finding ways to improve relations.

The meetings were facilitated by Susan Collin Marks, who possessed rare talents in making people feel comfortable and getting them to yes. We wanted the facilitation to provide an aura of impartiality, so we introduced Susan as a South African (which she was) and therefore neither an Iranian nor an American. To her credit, Susan quickly created an atmosphere that enabled participants to connect with each other. She guided the group past the stereotyping and demonization of the sort that had made me initially wary of Mahallati. Participants interacted on an equal and respectful basis.

We did our utmost to be culturally sensitive. We knew that the Iranian participants would not, as good Muslims, drink alcohol, so our first impulse was not to serve any alcoholic beverages at meals or even at the opening reception. But one of our American participants, a conservative think tanker, said that not being able to drink wine with his dinner discriminated against him. We queried the Iranians, and they agreed it would be fine to give this man a carafe of wine at meals even though everyone else was served juice and water. That solved the problem.

Knowing that most Iranians have a particular fondness for poetry, we started meetings with readings by the famed Persian poet Rumi and by Robert Frost, whose *Road Not Taken* seemed especially appropriate to those of us who wanted to move U.S.-Iranian relations down a new path. And we followed the maxim that had guided us in earlier sessions with Soviets and Middle Easterners. Instead of participants facing each other across the table as adversaries, they sat together and took on a shared problem: How to improve relations between the United States and Iran.

Susan had a cofacilitator—the Lebanese man who had put his arm around an Israeli general and declared him to be a friend at our first Middle Eastern meeting. This man spoke fluent Farsi, and he was the grandson of a famous Iranian ayatollah. One of his key roles was to find out from Iranian participants if and when they had problems with the process. During breaks he would walk around the nearby lake with them, and they would let him know what, if anything, was bothering them. They understood he was passing on what they said to Susan and our team, but they seemed to prefer talking to this man in Farsi rather than complaining directly to us in English. For instance, the Iranians told him that the process seemed to be one-sided because the Americans were asking most of the questions and the Iranians were mainly providing answers. The Iranians did not feel that the playing field was level, and they were not learning as much from the Americans as the Americans were learning from them. This had not been apparent to the U.S. participants who were simply curious about life and politics inside Iran, which had been mostly closed to them in the years since the country's 1979 revolution.

Clearly this perceived inequality needed to be rectified, so the American participants came up with a creative solution that was dubbed the *Paula Jones briefing*. At that time, Paula Jones was in the headlines for having claimed to have had an affair with President Bill Clinton, and our briefing was a gossipy way of providing the Iranians with what seemed to be the inside scoop on what was happening in Washington, D.C. It gave the Iranians juicy material on which they could dine out back in Tehran, even though they had to keep their participation at the meetings secret.

Each meeting lasted three days, and during the first thirteen months we had three meetings. Participants got to know each other, and friendships were born that exist to this day. At the third meeting, participants reached consensus around a *grand bargain* for improving relations. Included were ways to deal with issues related to frozen assets, expropriated property, security, narcotics, and culture. Participants felt good that they had been able to identify what they considered to be large areas of agreement. Thus they were subsequently disappointed when they went home and found that the policymakers in both governments were unreceptive to the compromises the group had laboriously worked out.

In Track 2 diplomacy, a rejection of this sort is called a *reentry problem*. It occurs when unofficial negotiators such as our participants get too far ahead of what their official counterparts are willing to accept. In fact, negotiators have been killed because they agreed to proposals that were unacceptable to their base back home. Fortunately, our participants received only a *not now* reaction as opposed to a violent one.

Nevertheless, because of the lack of official buy-in, participants were dispirited when they came back to Sweden in January 1998 for the fourth meeting. Then one of the Iranians, an inventive professor, proposed a different approach. He suggested that the time might be ripe for Americans to return to Tehran, where they had not openly appeared since the U.S.

Embassy was seized almost twenty years earlier. He noted that the presence of any Americans who came to Iran would be heavily criticized by hard-liners, but those who would be criticized the least would be wrestlers. Why wrestlers? In Iranian folklore, wrestlers are the great mythic heroes. They are, in essence, the samurai of Iran, and wrestling remains the most popular sport with the masses.

My colleagues and I were intrigued. We quickly recognized that sports might provide a good way to start bridging the gap between Iran and the United States, and that *wrestling diplomacy* might become the equivalent of what *ping-pong diplomacy* had been a quarter-century earlier between the United States and China. Taking American wrestlers to Iran seemed like a plausible, culturally appropriate means of moving forward without directly confronting the heart of the conflict. Our process had hit an obstacle, and wrestling diplomacy seemed to offer a path around it. Setbacks in peacemaking—as in life—do not justify giving up. Rather, they call for finding alternative routes forward.

Although I am an avid sports fan, I knew virtually nothing about wrestling. Nevertheless, I was willing to give it a try. After returning to Washington, D.C., I managed to make contact with USA Wrestling, America's national wrestling federation. I learned that it had previously received an invitation to send a team to Tehran to take part in a major tournament called the Takhti Cup, but that it was inclined not to accept. I quickly realized that my best option would be to convince USA Wrestling to compete in the tournament.

I discovered that the main barrier to participation for USA Wrestling had little to do with Iran or wrestling—and much to do with what had happened two years earlier when the organization had been widely criticized for taking several million dollars in contributions from John du Pont, a very rich wrestling aficionado and an heir to the du Pont chemical fortune. For the previous decade, du Pont had provided training and resident facilities for America's best wrestlers at Foxcatcher, his estate in rural Pennsylvania. Then in 1996, for reasons that have never been clear, he had shot and killed Dave Schultz, an Olympic gold medal–winning wrestler who had lived and coached at Foxcatcher. Subsequently, USA Wrestling had been accused of negligence because it had ignored du Pont's mental problems and put the wrestlers at risk in order to access du Pont's money and state of the art facilities. (This sordid tale of du Pont and the wrestlers was the subject of the 2014 Academy Award–nominated film *Foxcatcher*.)

Given this history, it was clear to me that the key to getting the leaders of USA Wrestling to agree to send their team to Iran was to convince them that the wrestlers would be safe and that no one would be criticized for endangering the wrestlers. That brought out my chutzpah—a Yiddish word meaning nerve or gall that is characteristic of most social entrepreneurs (see chapter 10)—and I offered USA Wrestling a partnership in which we at Search would look after the security and the politics, and USA Wrestling would take care of the wrestling.

USA Wrestling began to come around after I heard from State Department officials that they had "no objection" to the American wrestlers traveling to Iran. In diplomat speak, this meant that State gave its tacit approval while maintaining official separation. In addition, I arranged a meeting between USA Wrestling's leadership and the Iranian ambassador to the UN, at which the ambassador provided assurances that, as guests in Iran, the wrestlers would be completely safe. I also secured the support of the Swiss government, which represented U.S. interests in Iran. As a final touch, I provided USA Wrestling officials with the private phone number of the Swiss ambassador in Tehran and assured them that he would provide assistance in case of trouble. All of these efforts had the desired effect, and the leaders of USA Wrestling decided not only to send the team but also to go to Iran themselves.

Wrestling is a minor sport in America, and USA Wrestling officials told me they hoped that a high-visibility appearance in Iran would help make it into a major one. They believed the visit would attract considerable attention because it would be the first time in nearly twenty years that an American team in any sport had competed in Iran. They felt that the trip offered a way to popularize their sport. Doing so was not my top priority, although I certainly did not object to it. My main motive for organizing the trip was to improve relations between the United States and Iran. USA Wrestling and I were backing the same initiative for different reasons, which is often the case among people who are working together.

Once again, we were blessed with fortuitous timing. A month before the wrestlers left for Tehran, Iran's newly elected president, Mohammad Khatami, gave an interview to CNN in which he called for a "dialogue of civilizations" between Iran and the West. That made our initiative even more relevant, and my colleagues and I realized we now had a larger context within which wrestling diplomacy could move forward. With the wind in our sails, I flew off with Bill Kirby to Tehran to join the wrestlers.

I had been issued an Iranian entry visa as an *official*. Obviously, I was not an official in the governmental sense. The Iranians admitted me as an official of the sort who pounds the mat and shouts "one, two, three" at wrestling matches.

The American wrestlers who went to Iran had more authentic credentials. They included a former Olympic champion and two former world champions, and they turned out to be extraordinary people—as both sportsmen and citizen diplomats (figure 4.1). Having reached the peak in their sport, they were delighted to have a chance to make history. When they arrived in Tehran, two hundred reporters met them at the airport. They had never before been in a country where they were idolized *because* they were wrestlers. One of them said that now he thought he understood how it felt to be Michael Jordan and to play basketball in Chicago for the Bulls.

Mahallati met me in Tehran and showed me around (figure 4.2). Among other places, he took me to Tehran's central bazaar where I bought a small rug that still rests on the floor of my office. He and I ate lunch at a famous restaurant in the middle of the bazaar. We sat at a long, communal table to which merchants came to take their meals. Mahallati ordered Iranian

FIGURE 4.1 Former World and Olympic Champion Kevin Jackson, John Marks, and former World Champion Melvin Douglas III in Tehran.

FIGURE 4.2 *Washington Post* reporter Kenneth Cooper, John Marks, Amir Mahallati, and Bill Kirby at the Ayatollah Ruhollah Khomeini Mausoleum in Tehran.

delicacies and translated for me. Each time a new shopkeeper or trader sat down, he introduced me as an American. Admittedly, I was exposed to a very small sample of Iranians, but I was amazed by how pleased they were to meet me. In my view, their welcome went well beyond politeness, and I heard not a trace of anti-American rhetoric. When I said I had come with the American wrestling team, several people said, "It's about time."

The following day at the sports arena, the crowd greeted the U.S. wrestlers with similar warmth. There was heavy media coverage, and most of the newspaper, TV, and radio pieces focused on the return of Americans to Iran and the fact that the American flag was being openly displayed. Bringing the flag back to Iran was one of the major successes of our initiative. Although this had not been part of my initial to-do list, it was another example of how unforeseen results were often as important as the expected ones.

Here is what happened. Several days before the wrestlers were scheduled to leave for Tehran, I received a call from a USA Wrestling official. He asked if the wrestlers should take American flags with them. I hadn't thought about it, so I did what any good mediator would do, I deflected his question with a question: Did American wrestlers normally show the flag when they competed in international tournaments? The official answered that the flag was usually displayed whenever and wherever the national team competed. In my new role as a wrestling advisor, I then recommended that the team bring flags but only display them if the Iranians did not object. When we got to Tehran, the Iranians had no problem with the American flag being flown. I wrote later in the *Los Angeles Times*, "The American flag returned to Iran last week with honor, without chauvinism, and in an atmosphere of mutual respect."

The reappearance of the flag in Tehran became a major part of the story (figures 4.3 and 4.4). It fit perfectly with our evolving strategy of using wrestling diplomacy as a first step in improving U.S.-Iranian relations. For a new reality to take hold, I believed Americans needed to update and reframe their memories of the hostage crisis when hostile Iranian mobs repeatedly burned the flag. That image was deeply seared into America's collective consciousness. I wanted to expose a mass audience to very different pictures—of strong, proud American and Iranian athletes marching together behind the flag and even hugging each other. Because the global media showed up in large numbers in Tehran and the Iranians overwhelmingly welcomed the wrestlers, tens of millions of people were able to view these images of what might be possible.

FIGURE 4.3 The flag returns to Tehran.

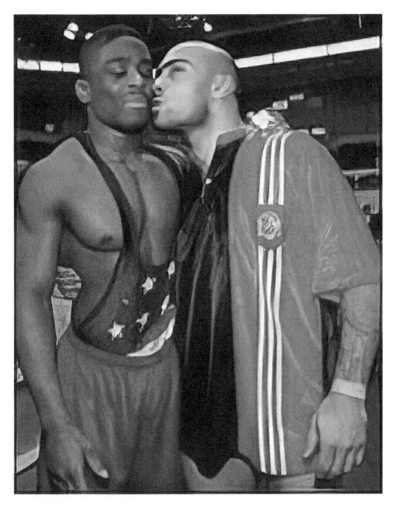

FIGURE 4.4 Wrestlers embrace.

For a fundamental shift to occur in U.S.-Iranian relations, both sides would also need to make major changes in the substance of their policies. But substance can be profoundly affected by powerful imagery that alters the very framework of an issue. The result can be a transformation of perceptions (see chapter 9).

I had never attended a defining sporting event, such as the finals of the soccer World Cup or the baseball World Series, but for me the 1998 Takhti Cup in Tehran proved to be just that. There were 13,000 spectators packed into a 12,000-seat arena. Most had come to see the Americans. Whenever a U.S. wrestler competed, the place became electric. The crowd was torn between rooting for Iranians to win and wanting to show approval of their American guests. The fans cheered for both, although the noise seemed a little louder for the Iranians. They roared when Zeke Jones won a silver medal and waved the Iranian flag afterward. There was a moment of disappointment when Kevin Jackson defeated an Iranian opponent, but that was followed by a huge ovation when the two wrestlers shared a long embrace. And the fans loved it when Jackson took a victory lap around the arena, high-fiving spectators as he ran.

In the last match, Melvin Douglas III opposed Abbas Jadidi, who had narrowly missed a gold medal at the 1996 Olympics because of a referee's controversial decision. The crowd kept shouting "Ja-di-di, Ja-di-di." He was clearly the hometown favorite. He and Douglas faced off in an epic struggle. Neither could gain a real edge, and at the end of regulation time, they were tied 3–3. With only a minute left in overtime, Jadidi managed to get behind Douglas and pick up his legs. Douglas struggled to escape. For twenty agonizing seconds Douglas showed almost superhuman resolve in not being flipped. Finally, Jadidi succeeded in turning over the American and won the match. Exhausted, the wrestlers collapsed on the mat and then quickly rose to hug each other. With their embrace, there was a huge surge of emotion. The crowd screamed the familiar refrain, "Ja-di-di, Ja-di-di." But they alternated it with "Doug-las, Doug-las."

Jadidi carried a large portrait of Iran's first Supreme Leader, Ayatollah Ruhollah Khomeini, as he walked to the podium to accept his medal. Douglas followed him holding a photograph of the current Supreme Leader, Ayatollah Ali Khamenei. The fans roared their support. At the beginning of the match, this same crowd had loudly demonstrated its disapproval for Ali Akbar Nateq-Nouri, the defeated, hardline presidential candidate who sat in the box of honor. Now they appreciated Douglas's gesture of respect toward the Islamic Republic. (Afterward I asked Douglas how he came to carry Khamenei's picture. He said that Jadidi asked him to do so, and he did not want to refuse.)

After the American wrestlers, Bill Kirby, and I had returned from Iran, we at Search decided to make Jadidi and Douglas winners of that year's Common Ground Award to honor them for their exemplary sportsmanship. Jadidi was unable to travel to Washington, D.C. for the ceremony, but he did get to visit New York. In front of an enthusiastic audience of Iranian-Americans in a mosque in Queens, I presented the trophy to

Jadidi and talked about the virtues of better relations between Iran and the United States.

Douglas came to both our awards ceremony and a visit I arranged for the wrestlers at the White House with President Clinton (figure 4.5). The trip to the Oval Office occurred because, on a long shot, I inquired whether the president, who was a big sports fan, might want to meet the wrestlers. I made contact through Sandy Berger, the president's National Security Advisor. Berger had been a student with me at Cornell, although I had hardly known him. Also, his daughter and my son had been classmates at the same elementary school in Washington, D.C., and he and I had talked a few times at school functions. Thus he had a sense of who I was, and I felt comfortable contacting him at the White House. When I telephoned, I did not get through, so I left him a voicemail explaining what I wanted. A few days later, somewhat to my surprise, I received a call from the White House scheduling office to arrange a meeting. If I had not been able to take advantage of my connection to Berger, however obscure, the wrestlers and

FIGURE 4.5 President Clinton greets John Marks and the U.S. national wrestling team as National Security Advisor Sandy Berger (left) and wrestler Melvin Douglas (right) look on.

I almost certainly would not have been invited to meet the president. The lesson here for social entrepreneurs is to make maximum use of connections, no matter how distant.

Our invitation to the Oval Office was motivated by the fact—of which I had no prior knowledge—that the president wanted to send a positive signal to Iran. As always, it was much easier to ride a horse in the direction it was going. The wrestlers, USA Wrestling officials, Bill Kirby, and I were graciously welcomed by the president. In addition, we invited former hostage Bruce Laingen to join us (figure 4.6). His participation was an added bonus, and it caused the *Los Angeles Times* to write that "Laingen's presence showed the support of former hostages for U.S. reconciliation with Iran."

The White House arranged for the U.S. government's Worldnet satellite TV network to film our visit to the Oval Office and broadcast the proceedings to Iran. The idea was to send a signal about the possibility of better

FIGURE 4.6 From left: William Kirby, Bruce Reider (team doctor), John Marks, John Giura (wrestler), Mitch Hull (USA Wrestling, national teams director), Shawn Charles (wrestler), President Bill Clinton, Larry Sciacchetano (USA Wrestling president), Zeke Jones (wrestler), James Scherr (USA Wrestling executive director), Melvin Douglas (wrestler), Bruce Laingen (former ambassador, hostage in Iran 1979–1981), and James McCord (referee).

relations. To make sure the Iranians got the message, White House Press Secretary Mike McCurry stated this at a press briefing:

> It would be accurate to say that [President Clinton is] drawing attention to an exchange, a people-to-people exchange, that is maybe off the beaten path of diplomacy, but it has something to say about the prospect and hope for more beneficial relations between peoples.

As Track 2 practitioners, we prided ourselves on being "off the beaten path," and we were hugely pleased that the president saw fit to use our work to tee up his approach to the Iran issue. From our perspective, this was as good as it gets. Wrestling diplomacy had provided a vivid new context in which to think about the possibility of better relations between Iran and the United States. It had created an extended metaphor that went like this: Wrestlers from the two countries competed fiercely, but within mutually accepted rules. Both sides recognized that differences existed, but they allowed their common humanity to triumph.

After this event, we Searchers faced an operational dilemma. Our meetings in Sweden had been conducted in great secrecy, whereas our involvement in wrestling had been showcased by global media and then by the White House. As pleased as we were by the positive attention, we had lost the ability to carry out our work with Iran in secret. We decided to make a virtue out of necessity and adopted a two-track strategy: (1) we would sponsor public exchanges that involved Iranians and Americans, and (2) we would continue to hold confidential meetings.

On the exchange front, we were convinced that a rapid growth in non-official, people-to-people visits in both directions could make a major contribution to lessening the combustibility of U.S.-Iranian relations. Although we knew that only governments could make peace, history had shown—from the Cold War to the Oslo process to South Africa's transition from apartheid to democracy—that Track 2 activities could make a real difference. At the same time, activities (such as wrestling) that were successful in one country would not necessarily work in other places, and we recognized that a high level of cultural sensitivity was required in the design of activities.

In addition, we knew we needed to be attentive to some wise words from Rudolf Weiersmüller, the Swiss ambassador in Tehran. In addition to being a former wrestler himself, he had a great deal of experience interacting with Americans and Iranians because he frequently served as the middleman in indirect talks between the governments. He told us that he saw a basic difference in negotiating styles between the two sides. In his view, Americans were like a U.S. football team: they were ready to forget past results, march down the field, and make immediate scores. In contrast, Iranians were like chess players (ancient Persians having invented the game). They developed complex strategies, took nothing on face value, and planned ahead a dozen moves. Ambassador Weiersmüller noted that these very different approaches represented a major barrier to better relations.

During the next few years, we carried out a series of public exchanges to help bridge the gap. We wanted to build a web of high-profile relationships (figure 4.7). To this end, we organized two Iranian-American cinema summits on the sidelines of the Cannes Film Festival; we sponsored showings of Iranian movies at the Kennedy Center and the Smithsonian Institution in Washington, D.C.; we arranged for *An Inconvenient Truth*, the Academy Award–winning documentary on global warming, to be shown in Iran; we took American astronauts Rusty Schweickart and Bruce McCandless to Iran and arranged reciprocal visits of scientists, environmentalists,

FIGURE 4.7 Ambassador Thomas Pickering, Professor Rouhollah Ramazani, and Foreign Minister Javad Zarif.

FIGURE 4.8 Astronaut Bruce McCandless (center) shows visiting Iranian scientists the American West.

academics, and doctors (figure 4.8); we even cosponsored an Iranian art exhibit in the United States (figure 4.9). One exchange of which I was especially proud occurred when we brought a delegation of six female Iranian filmmakers to the United States. The idea was to spotlight the work of these highly skilled *cinéastes* and to have their professionalism fly in the face of existing stereotypes about Iranian women. They screened their films at Lincoln Center and the Council on Foreign Relations in New York and at the Art Institute of Chicago.

We even tried *eclipse diplomacy* in 1999 when Alan Hale (codiscoverer of the Hale-Bopp comet) asked if we could arrange to bring a scientific delegation to Iran to observe the last solar eclipse of the millennium. He said that Isfahan in Iran would be the best place on the planet to watch. Although we had never contemplated an astronomical foray, we operated from the premise that success in building bridges required innovation. We found an able Iranian host, the Zirakzadeh Scientific Society, and we put together a group that included twelve Americans. We even got NASA to provide a stunning photograph taken by the Hubble Space Telescope to be presented to Iranian leaders. In addition to viewing the eclipse, the

FIGURE 4.9 Painting from Iranian art exhibit that toured the United States.

American delegation made presentations at scientific institutions where, in Dr. Bopp's words, they were greeted "like rock stars"—as the American wrestlers had been.

In all, we sponsored more than forty exchanges and other events between Iranians and their American counterparts. For better or worse, we became the most active U.S. organization working to build better relations between Iran and the United States. We found it difficult to make much of an impression in the United States, but the Iranians paid careful attention. As Nasser Hadian of Tehran University said, "What [Search for Common Ground] has been doing has had a profound effect on the psyche of both the [Iranian] public and the elite. . . . No other activities have had such an effect." Indeed, in 2000, the hardline Tehran newspaper *Lesarat*—which did not intend to pay us a compliment—wrote, "Informed sources say that a very important organization is active in America, called "Research on Common Grounds" [sic] . . . Most of the activities in connection with Iran are first planned in that organization."

Both the Clinton and Khatami administrations showed considerable interest in improving relations, but these efforts failed for a variety of reasons involving national egos, opposition from hard-liners in both countries, and the failure of the two governments to pay sufficient attention to the needs of the other. In the end, neither government was willing to expend the political capital necessary to take advantage of the openings. There was a brief respite in 2001 after 9/11. With George W. Bush in the White House, the Iranians offered to cooperate in a shared effort to prevent terrorism, and they worked in tandem with the United States in installing a post-Taliban government in Afghanistan. However, in January 2002 Bush famously asserted that Iran was part of the "axis of evil," and Iranian leaders became equally harsh in describing the United States. After that the relationship turned completely sour.

As relations worsened, Bill Miller, our senior advisor for Iran, became a principal conduit between the two countries. Before Iran's 1979 revolution, Miller had spent five years there as a U.S. diplomat, and he had developed a profound love for the country and its culture. After Khomeini seized power in 1979, President Jimmy Carter asked Miller to be the U.S. ambassador to Iran, but before he could be confirmed the U.S. Embassy in Tehran was seized by militant students. Needless to say, Miller was never able to take up the post, although he was very much involved in negotiations to free the American hostages. After 444 days of captivity, the hostages were released, but diplomatic relations were never resumed. In 1993, President Clinton appointed Miller U.S. ambassador to Ukraine. He stepped down in 1997 and joined Search to work on Iran. He proved to be a superb Track 2 diplomat.

After Mahmoud Ahmadinejad became Iran's president in 2005, we found it virtually impossible to obtain visas for U.S. participants in our exchanges. On several occasions, we had to cancel trips at the last minute because the Iranian Foreign Ministry had not issued the necessary entry permits. (I used to joke that the concept of a nonrefundable airline ticket could not be translated into the Farsi language.) We had little choice but to de-emphasize exchanges, and we concentrated on arranging high-level meetings between Iranians and Americans that were focused on the nuclear issue.

Our assumption was that someday negotiations on nuclear matters would be necessary between Iran and the United States, and a host of issues would have to be resolved for those talks to be successful. With relations at a low point, we also realized that neither government was likely to seriously consider the particulars of a future agreement. Thus in 2005 we launched the U.S.-Iran Nuclear Initiatives Group. Participants included top Iranian and American experts on nuclear questions and people with policymaking experience, including a UN nuclear inspector, a former chief negotiator on nuclear issues for Iran, a hydrogen bomb designer, and several others with similar credentials. The group focused on providing impartial analysis and limited its work to technical issues. The goals were to make available to policymakers in both countries specific ways to strengthen the nonproliferation regime and to contribute creative ideas to an eventual negotiation process.

From 2005 to 2007, the Nuclear Initiatives Group met on six occasions with Javad Zarif, then Iran's ambassador to the UN. Zarif later became foreign minister, and he personally negotiated the eventual nuclear agreement (the Joint Comprehensive Plan of Action or JCPOA). In addition, Miller met privately with Zarif about once a month. Here is what Zarif had to say about our role during this period:

> I believe you saved our negotiations. . . . Without the work of the group, I believe discussions would have ended. . . . If there is any outcome of the negotiations that is to the satisfaction of both sides, it will be a derivative of the discussions of this group.

When Barack Obama became president of the United States in 2009, new possibilities emerged. Miller arranged for and attended confidential meetings in Europe and New York between former U.S. Secretary of Defense William Perry and Ali Akbar Salehi, then head of Iran's Atomic Energy Organization. Both men had access to top-level policymakers. We never learned what Salehi told Iranian leaders, but we knew that Perry reported directly to President Obama his conclusion that agreements on nuclear issues were possible. Miller believed that this was a key first step toward moving the United States into the negotiations with Iran that resulted in the eventual signing of a nuclear agreement.

FIGURE 4.10 From left: Marvin Miller, nuclear scientist; Olli Heinonen, former deputy director, IAEA; Frank von Hippel, a Princeton University physicist; Ali Akhbar Salehi, former head of Iranian Atomic Energy Organization; Rush Holt, former U.S. Congressman and a physicist; and Ambassador Bill Miller at a meeting after signing of the JCPOA. All were participants in Search's Nuclear Initiatives Group.

While the official talks were underway, members of Search's Nuclear Initiatives Group (figure 4.10) collaborated on detailed technical papers on how to overcome possible obstacles to concluding agreements. Particularly important was a plan authored by three participants—Frank von Hippel, Hossein Mousavian, and Alex Glaser—to redesign the Arak heavy water reactor into a device with far less yield of plutonium and to convert 20 percent enriched uranium into fuel plates. This paper, which was given to both Iranian and American negotiators, provided the basis on which the issue was eventually resolved. As Foreign Minister Zarif said in 2016:

> I have used what I learned from you when we last met in the negotiations, particularly on conversion of the fuel to oxide form, the limit of the number of centrifuges, and conversion of the Arak reactor. . . . Thank you for shaping my thinking from the very beginning in how this could be resolved. . . . You can claim parenthood in this endeavor. Thank you for putting the road in place for us to follow.

Zarif's American negotiating partner, Secretary of State John Kerry, similarly stated in a 2017 filmed interview: "During the Iran talks, the fresh ideas you provided helped us to achieve a breakthrough on the Arak heavy water reactor."

As a result of more than two decades of showing up with Iran, we had developed numerous contacts—from the foreign minister down—on nuclear matters and other political questions. As a result, when opportunities presented themselves, we often were able to move things forward. For instance, when three American hikers wandered across the Iraq-Iran border in 2011 and were arrested, we were approached by two of their mothers who had heard that we had good connections with Iranian officials. Although one hiker, a young woman, had already been freed, the two mothers hoped that our unofficial, Track 2 intervention might assist in getting their sons released from Tehran's notorious Evin Prison. We agreed, and Bill Miller used his regular meetings with Iranian officials in New York and Europe to seek the release of the two young men who were being held.

Miller understood that he was not going to be able to convince the Iranians that the hikers should be released before their top leadership decided it was time to do so. However, he believed he might be able to hasten a decision by making things easier for them. As Track 2 practitioners, we try to be win-win problem-solvers. We are not bound by governmental procedures and protocols and often have more leeway to explore possibilities that traditional diplomats would be less likely to pursue.

It is obvious to us that parties in negotiation almost never reach agreement for the same reasons, and that they virtually always act in ways that they believe serve their best interests—which are invariably different from those of the people with whom they are negotiating. Moreover, solutions need to be found that allow participants to save face. In the case of the hikers, when the moment came for the Iranians to free them, we realized it would be important to Iranian leaders that they should not be seen as having caved to U.S. government pressure. Therefore, we suggested that the Iranians might release the hikers to the care of American clergymen—specifically Bishop John Chane, the former Episcopal Bishop of Washington, D.C., and Cardinal Theodore McCarrick, former Catholic Archbishop of Washington, D.C. (who was subsequently defrocked because of his alleged involvement in sexual abuse cases). Most of the top Iranian leaders were clerics themselves, and we thought that dealing with American religious leaders would make it easier for them to release the hikers.

Miller kept gently pressing the Iranians and providing them with ideas. One day in September 2011 his phone rang, and he was told that Iranian officials had decided to free the hikers and we should immediately send the cardinal and the bishop, as well as a prominent American Moslem leader, to Iran to receive the prisoners. We were thrilled, but first a series of logistical problems had to be overcome.

Normally it took months to arrange Iranian visas even for prominent Americans like the bishop and the cardinal, and more often than not the Iranians turned down the applications. In this case, we were told we could pick up visas for the two clergymen within a few days. Then there was the question of who was going to pay for the hikers' plane tickets from Tehran back to the United States. We were relatively sure the Iranians would not be willing to do so, and we knew the hikers would not be able to pay for their own tickets. We had visions of them being stranded at Tehran's airport and realized that Search would probably have to be the banker for this mission. We reasoned that the bishop and the cardinal needed to carry enough cash to Tehran to buy, if necessary, one-way business class tickets for the hikers, which would cost about $5,000 each.

Why business class? Search was—and is—a frugal, nonprofit organization whose staff is obligated to fly economy class. But the hikers had spent two years in a harsh Iranian prison, and it seemed wrong to skimp on bringing them home. As president of Search, I authorized an exception to our normal travel policy to allow the released prisoners to fly business class.

In addition, we knew that the tickets would need to be paid for in cash. Why cash? U.S. credit cards could not—and still cannot—be used in Iran because of American financial sanctions. The cardinal and the bishop would have to use cash to pay for the tickets and their hotel rooms. Also, we were mindful that there is a U.S. government requirement that anyone leaving the country with more than $10,000 must make a customs declaration. We did not think it would be a good idea for the bishop and the cardinal to have to justify their trip to customs officials, so in the best Solomonic tradition, we split the money in two so neither man would have to carry more than $10,000.[1]

The bishop was a member of Washington's stately Cosmos Club, and he arranged a private room where Miller and I could meet him and the cardinal to make final arrangements. We gave them their plane tickets and

---

1. We later learned that because both clergymen were traveling together and the money was from one source our bright idea of dividing the money between them did not overcome the requirement to declare the funds. Thus our strategy of splitting the money in two was too clever by half, but no federal agents ever bothered us about it.

photo : Mohammad Hassanzadeh

FIGURE 4.11 Foreign Minister Javad Zarif greets Cardinal McCarrick and Bishop Chane in Tehran.

two envelopes, each containing $6,000 in hundred-dollar bills—$5,000 for each hiker's plane ticket and $1,000 to pay for hotels and meals. The cardinal and the bishop were both amused and understanding about the need for cash, and they signed receipts for the money. The bishop remarked that Search must have a very understanding finance department because he was sure that he never could have convinced his own diocesan comptroller to approve a cash transaction of this kind.

The two clerics left for Tehran four days later (figure 4.11). They were accompanied by Nihad Awad, the head of the Council on American-Islamic Relations (CAIR). While they were changing planes in Istanbul, President Obama telephoned to wish them well in Tehran. The cardinal and the bishop had met with President Mahmoud Ahmadinejad the year before in New York, and they had prayed together for peace. At that time, the cardinal and the bishop had asked Ahmadinejad for compassionate intervention regarding the hikers. This time when they met Ahmadinejad told them, according to Bishop Chane, "It was because of our presence that they were able to move the process forward in releasing the hikers."

In addition to our Track 2 efforts, Track 1 government officials from two other countries were involved in freeing the hikers. The late Sultan Qaboos of Oman played a critical role in convincing the Iranians to consider the strategic utility, as well as the religious imperative, of releasing the hikers, who had committed no crime. And the Swiss government also played an important part.

In the end, we did not have to pay for the hikers' airline tickets because the Omani government provided a plane to fly the hikers out of Iran. To the benefit of our organizational treasury, the Iranian government also paid for hotel rooms in Tehran for the cardinal and the bishop. Search got back the entire $12,000 we had advanced, and our only cost was for the plane tickets for the bishop and the cardinal (figure 4.12), who also flew business class.

We had kept White House and State Department officials informed of what we were doing, and they had privately urged us to continue our unofficial efforts. Through our persistence, we had become prime inter- locutors between Iran and the United States because the two governments were not talking to each other in any meaningful way at that time. When

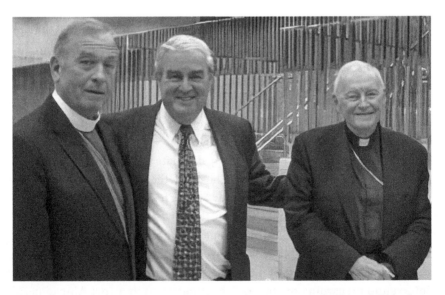

FIGURE 4.12 Ambassador Bill Miller (center) welcomes Bishop Chane (left) and Cardinal McCarrick (right) at Dulles Airport when they returned from Tehran on September 20, 2011.

governments are communicating well, there is much less space for Track 2 organizations like ours. The opening for our involvement usually depends on there being a high degree of animosity between the parties. We would prefer not to be bottom feeders for whom opportunities increase as conflict intensifies, but unfortunately we tend to be called upon when official relations are at their worst. The world would be a much better place if there were less demand for our services.

Nevertheless, by showing up on Iran, particularly before governments were willing to act, we were able to plant the seeds for what we hoped would be much bigger things to come. Our involvement provided a testing ground for innovative ideas and joint problem-solving. We helped build trust, which was necessary if relations were ever going to improve. We created a certain number of openings that Track 1 officials in both countries might have taken greater advantage of if they had possessed the political will, which they did not—and still do not.

5

Enroll Credible Supporters

In addition to showing up, social entrepreneurs need to project credibility. One important way to do this is to activate Principle #5, "enroll credible supporters." Successful social entrepreneurs should be able to convince the outside world that they will achieve what they say they will. Credibility is best gained by doing good work and having a reputation for so doing, but social entrepreneurs can increase the odds in their favor by *borrowing* credibility from prestigious people. This is especially true when budding entrepreneurs are not yet well-known and are developing new ventures.

There are dangers, however, with this borrowing tactic. Social entrepreneurs need to be cautious about bringing in powerful people who are not aligned with their vision or who are inclined to commandeer the work of others. In their quest to enroll credible supporters, entrepreneurs should be careful not to lose control of their organization or to act in ways that lack integrity. Particularly perilous are strong-minded outsiders who prefer to do things their own way and who have time on their hands. As the head of another NGO once warned me about selecting new board members, "Be sure to stay away from people who don't have enough to do."

The key is to enroll distinguished individuals who are willing to be supportive—or at least who are not controlling or oppositional. That being said, here are some specific ways for social entrepreneurs to enhance their credibility.

- **Put well-known people on your board of directors and on your advisory board.** The first chair of Search's board was Patricia Aburdene. Her husband at the time, the late John Naisbitt, also served on the board. Together this dynamic couple wrote the *Megatrends* books (although Patricia only received credit as coauthor of *Megatrends 2000*). These books were huge bestsellers that described what John and Patricia saw to be the trends that were reshaping the planet. Search's credibility was definitely enhanced when the *Naisburdenes* (as the two of them were collectively called) proclaimed publicly that searching for common ground represented a megatrend. In addition, they introduced us to people who were of considerable help to the organization, and they provided us with a series of good ideas that greatly contributed to our work. Above all, by having them as board members, we were able to project an image of being on the cutting edge of global thinking.
- **Seek publicity for your accomplishments, but don't overdo it.** Favorable attention can put an entrepreneurial venture on the map, but too much or unwarranted or premature self-promotion can be detrimental. Social entrepreneurs should avoid being criticized for being publicity hounds. I adopted a policy of not talking publicly about future projects until I was reasonably certain that they were actually going to happen. For example, I waited until I knew for sure that the American wrestling team would be traveling to Iran before I alerted the media, and then I did it discreetly—not by issuing a press release but by going to an acquaintance at the *Washington Post* and offering an exclusive to the paper if it sent a journalist to Tehran to cover the tournament. The *Post*'s editors agreed, and they assigned the story to their reporter Kenneth Cooper. However, my caution caused a problem. Because I had waited until almost the last minute before making arrangements, through no fault of his own Cooper was late in applying for a visa from Iran's slow bureaucracy. Fortunately, on the last possible day he could have traveled without missing the wrestling tournament, he received his visa—thanks to one of the Iranian participants in our U.S.-Iran Working Group who expedited the issuing process. Cooper reached Iran just in time, and he wound up writing two articles for the *Post* that included mention of our role in launching wrestling diplomacy. Nevertheless, I was not able to provide the *Post* with the exclusive coverage I had promised it would receive. Although I kept my word and didn't alert any

other media outlets, the global press learned the Americans were coming to Tehran from the Iranian side and from USA Wrestling. As a result, international reporters showed up in large numbers. Fortunately, no one at the *Post* complained, and the huge amount of media attention we received turned out to be very helpful for Search.

• **Don't bad-mouth others.** In the course of their careers, social entrepreneurs make contact with hundreds, if not thousands, of people and organizations. Their credibility is enhanced—or at least not damaged—if they can minimize outside criticism. A good way to avoid being a target—in addition to not doing anything to deserve it—is not to speak ill of others. This insight turned out to be particularly important to us at Search when we became relatively successful at fund-raising, which might have caused other organizations to resent us. In our field, we were the big boys and girls on the block, and we were susceptible to being disparaged by those whose organizations had not raised as much money as we had. For the most part, we avoided this by not sharing negative views of others and by being as helpful as possible whenever outsiders contacted us. Not only was this a good strategy, but it was also consistent with our core values.

• **Secure the services of distinguished people.** Even when well-known outsiders who are not control freaks share the vision of a social entrepreneur, bringing them into the organization often does not work. A lesson I learned the hard way was that former ambassadors do not necessarily make effective NGO employees. In general terms, no matter how renowned the individual, success in one career is not necessarily a predictor of what would happen in another. With this caution in mind, however, including the right people, when it works, can have a huge payoff. This is what happened after our Middle East initiative was approached by former U.S. Assistant Secretary of State and Ambassador to Egypt Alfred "Roy" Atherton (figure 5.1). Atherton was retired, had heard about our work, and made an unsolicited call to me, saying that he wanted to become involved. We had never before had such a high-level volunteer, and he became the chair of our Middle East Advisory Board. Similarly, we made another productive move in enrolling Peter Constable, a wise, silver-haired, former U.S. Ambassador to Zaire, as our Middle East project's first executive director. These two experienced diplomats came from a world of protocol and *démarches*. To join our free-flowing organization clearly required major leaps of faith on their part. They provided instant credibility for us, and they were among the few retired ambassadors who had the right skill sets for our work. In addition, they gave us standing on the Track 1 level at a time when many

FIGURE 5.1 Search Middle East advisory board chair, Ambassador Roy Atherton, meets with Egyptian President Hosni Mubarak.

people still saw us as a fringe organization. Their presence—with its implied endorsement—helped make it possible for us to receive significant increases in funding.

In Macedonia (now the Republic of North Macedonia) we opened our first ever field office in 1993, and the strategy of hiring an eminent outsider also worked well there. I had a direct experience of this when I visited Skopje, the capital city, for the first time, and I was taken directly from the airport to a private lunch with the country's president, the late Kiro Gligorov. I had never before been wined and dined by a head of state—nor would I ever be again. The reason it happened had little to do with me. It was because we had engaged the services of former U.S. Ambassador Robert Frowick to be our country director (figure 5.2). Frowick had been about to retire the year before when the Acting Secretary of State, Lawrence Eagleburger, asked him to accept an unorthodox mission involving Macedonia, which had just become a separate country with the breakup of Yugoslavia. At that point, Macedonia's independence was so new that no Western country had yet officially recognized it or sent an ambassador.

Frowick's assignment was to go to Skopje as the U.S. government's unofficial representative. Officially he represented the Conference for Security and Cooperation in Europe (CSCE), and he was given the cumbersome title Director of the Spill-Over Monitor Mission. In this capacity, he lacked most of the amenities and support a U.S. ambassador normally receives,

Search for Common Ground President John Marks and Macedonian
project Executive Director Robert Frowick meet with President
Gligorov of Macedonia.

J o S
Our first correspondence

FIGURE 5.2 John Marks, Search Country Director Ambassador Robert Frowick, and Macedonian President Kiro Gligorov just before they sat down for lunch.

but he was the highest ranking foreign official in the country, and he became, in effect, the Western proconsul. As such, he worked closely and effectively with President Gligorov to prevent ethnic violence. I used to compare him to the Marquis de Lafayette—that is to say, the foreigner who had the greatest impact in securing a country's independence.

After six months in his CSCE role, Frowick left Macedonia and went home to what he thought would be a peaceful retirement in northern California's wine country, but he remained hooked by Macedonia. Although I had never met him, he seemed to be exactly what we needed to launch our program, so I cold-called him. He was very impressive on the phone, and I wound up offering him the job as our country director in Skopje. He accepted. That made him Search's first full-time employee outside of Washington, D.C.

Frowick's goal was, as he put it, "to keep Macedonia from exploding." Search gave him a platform from which he could strengthen the country's immune system. He brought to the job an ambassadorial presence and impeccability. His trademark outfit was a white linen suit, which might have been designed by Halston, the famous fashion designer who happened to be his brother. And, of course, he still maintained the connections he had formed earlier, including his close relationship with President Gligorov. With Frowick's influence, Gligorov turned into an extremely credible supporter of Search, and our relationship with the president laid the groundwork for what became one of our most successful country programs. Having the president of the country in our corner certainly enhanced our credibility.

Macedonia provided a model for effective conflict prevention. Under the leadership of Frowick and our subsequent country directors, Search became a key player in what was a three-legged effort. The components were a small military peacekeeping force whose members wore the blue helmets of the UN, governmental foreign aid programs, and NGO actions such as ours. These three elements represented an exemplary mix of diplomatic, economic, military, psychological, and conflict resolution measures. However, probably the most important reason the country did not explode was that Macedonians were fully aware of the appalling violence in nearby Bosnia, and most of them—no matter what their ethnicity—did not want their country to suffer the same fate. In Macedonia, the bottom line was that the leadership, from the president on down, never allowed ethnic enmities to overwhelm them, and they mostly avoided demagoguery. Before things could get out of hand, they demonstrated sufficient political will to make compromises and resolve problems.

Our role in this violence-prevention campaign was to carry out projects to promote tolerance and build bridges between and among the country's various ethnic groups. One of our first efforts was to convene an interethnic training workshop for Macedonian journalists on how to report on conflict in accurate, noninflammatory ways. As so many NGOs have done before and since, that project involved taking a group of trainees to a resort hotel outside the capital city and bringing in foreign experts to instruct them. At the end of the workshop we asked participants to evaluate their experience; they said that they welcomed the chance to get away from their daily routines and relax in what was for them a luxurious setting, but they had heard much of what the trainers had to offer before. They advised that the training would have been considerably more effective if it had been more hands-on and tied to their actual work. Instead of their being told how to cover interethnic cooperation, they wanted a direct experience of actually reporting on it.

As a result of this feedback, we launched a new project to support team reporting involving the country's leading Slavic Macedonian, Albanian, and Turkish language newspapers. Each participating paper agreed to provide a journalist to coauthor articles with a journalist from another paper that was published in a different language and targeted a different ethnic group. The journalists carried out the investigation together, and their articles simultaneously appeared in their home newspapers under a joint byline. (Later we added pairs of reporters from TV and radio stations.)

At first we supplied editors from abroad who, we believed, would also function as mediators between the reporters. Denise Hamilton of the *Los Angeles Times* was the first such editor. Under her direction, an Albanian and an ethnic-Macedonian reporter worked together to research and coauthor a multipart series on the country's health care systems, a seemingly nonpolitical issue that affected almost everyone. The common ground turned out to be that most of the population suffered from a lack of reliable medical attention. Regardless of ethnicity, getting sick in Macedonia was not a good idea.

By working together as a team, the reporters were able to move beyond incendiary and stereotypical coverage of the *other*. In the process, their output minimized the tendency to incite conflict that was so prevalent in the Balkan region. After a few joint articles were written, the reporters found that they no longer needed an expatriate editor. Altogether this project produced more than sixty articles and three TV series that encouraged dialogue and mutual understanding. In addition, we continued to hold training and discussion programs for journalists.

Macedonia is a comparatively small country, and during those years we worked closely with virtually every newspaper, TV station, and radio outlet. As a direct result, during the Kosovo crisis in 1998–99 when Macedonia was on the brink of serious ethnic violence, the press was relatively restrained in its coverage and largely avoided descending into *hate media*, which had been prevalent in other parts of former Yugoslavia. In fact, two Macedonian radio stations that had been involved with us—one Albanian and the other ethnic-Macedonian—even shared information and worked together to debunk rumors. Although Macedonia experienced some violence, it never got out of hand, and the country stayed relatively peaceful. We were proud of the contribution we made in helping to keep the lid on violence. Our effort to promote tolerance certainly saved lives.

In 1994, Robert Frowick stepped down as our country director. He was replaced by Eran Fraenkel, an expert on the Balkans who was fluent in both Slavic Macedonian and Albanian—and who told us he could "get by" in Turkish. These were the country's three principal languages. Frowick certainly lent us his ambassadorial standing, but Fraenkel brought a different kind of credibility because he was so skilled on the linguistic and cultural fronts. He also brought his wife Edith and their two-year-old daughter, Sarah, with him. Unexpectedly, having his family with him greatly contributed to two of our most innovative projects.

At that time, all of Macedonia's schools were rigidly segregated by language, and the emphasis was on rote learning. Schools did not offer courses in which students could learn any local language except their parent tongue, although most people from ethnic minorities could speak Slavic Macedonian, the language of the majority. Bilingual classes were, in fact, illegal. Consequently, from early childhood on, a good number of people in the country had little or no contact with their fellow citizens from other ethnic groups. This kind of isolation perpetuated negative stereotypes that usually stayed with children into adulthood.

When Sarah Fraenkel was ready to start school, her parents had to decide whether they were going to send her to a Macedonian-language or an Albanian-language kindergarten. They would have much preferred a diverse, bilingual class, but they had to make a zero-sum choice and wound up enrolling her in a Macedonian-language school. When it was time to celebrate Sarah's third birthday, ethnic tensions in the country were particularly high, and the Fraenkels believed they could not safely hold a party for the children of both their Slavic Macedonian and Albanian friends.

Faced with what to them was an unpalatable choice, Edith had an insight. She declared that Search needed to do something to change things, and she suggested that the answer might be to start bilingual kindergartens.

Edith's vision took on concrete form shortly thereafter when Eran Fraenkel and Violeta Beška of the University of Skopje attended a conference in Norway. They heard two speakers—one Palestinian-Israeli and one Jewish-Israeli—describe how an organization inside Israel, Neve Shalom/Wahat al-Salam, ran a school where Hebrew and Arabic were coequal, and where the playing field was level for both ethnic groups. This was exactly the kind of early education system they had dreamt of creating in Macedonia. They approached the two speakers and secured their help in designing a curriculum and training materials for future kindergartens. A partnership was born between champions of ethnic coexistence in Macedonia and Israel.

Eran Fraenkel drafted a proposal to establish bilingual kindergartens, but he found that no funding was available from Macedonian sources. Neither were international donors initially supportive. But even if he had found the money quickly, nothing could have moved forward without convincing the Macedonian government to change the law that prohibited bilingual education. It took Fraenkel three years to get the interethnic kindergartens off the ground. He persuaded the Swiss government's foreign aid agency to provide funds, and he lobbied the Macedonian government to change the law forbidding bilingual education. (However, that change only applied to students of kindergarten age.) By the time he was able to move forward, his daughter was already too old to attend one of the new classes. But Fraenkel was not deterred, and he and his successors wound up creating a nationwide network of thirteen kindergartens that they called *Mozaik*. These classrooms played a key role in transforming early childhood education in Macedonia. For the first time ever, young children were able to interact and receive instruction in an inclusive, bilingual environment in which no ethnic group predominated and everyone was treated equally. Mozaik stressed joy and critical thinking, along with tolerance and conflict resolution. Here are some brief stories from Mozaik:

- Aleksandra, a Macedonian kindergartener, loves Ensar, an Albanian classmate. Aleksandra uses blocks to build both a mosque and a church. She says that she has placed the church next to the mosque so when she and Ensar marry, they will each be able to worship in nearby buildings.

- Veton and Christian spend hours playing and talking together, but they don't understand the other's language. Still they find ways to communicate, and they are the best of friends.
- Jana explains to classmates what the word "nostalgia" means: That is when you are at home, but you miss Mozaik and want to be there.
- According to a parent, her son Nikola always reminds the family of how they should behave at home—just like the children do at Mozaik.

After eight years with Search in Macedonia, the Fraenkels decided Sarah needed a broader education than she could receive in Skopje, so Search reassigned Eran Fraenkel to Brussels where Sarah could attend schools with more diverse opportunities. One of Fraenkel's successors as our Macedonian country director was Vilma Venkovska Milčev. She had been the first staff member hired by Frowick, and Mozaik was her passion. She was deeply convinced—both professionally and as a mother whose son was in the first Mozaik class—that Macedonia very much needed bilingual education. She also recognized that the Mozaik kindergartens would not survive in the long run unless they became part of the Macedonian public education system. The Swiss government had been extraordinarily generous and far-sighted in financing Mozaik for thirteen years, which was an unprecedented length of time for any international funder to stay with a project. But Milčev knew that even the Swiss would not continue forever, and she worked relentlessly to have the Macedonian government adopt the Mozaik kindergartens—and pay for them. The parents of students were hugely supportive, and the Mozaik classes had long waiting lists; however, Macedonia's educational establishment was resistant to change. Finally, in 2010 Milčev succeeded, and the Ministry of Labor and Social Policy agreed to assume ownership of Mozaik, with local governments taking on the costs, including the salaries of the teachers. Thus Mozaik ended its dependence on foreign funding and became both Macedonian and sustainable. This was the first Search project that was institutionalized by the host country.

Subsequently, the ministry expanded the program and opened many new classrooms while retaining most of the original model. In addition, Milčev took Mozaik to neighboring Kosovo, where it was replicated for ethnic Albanian and Serbian children in partnership with Save the Children.

In her struggle to make Mozaik a permanent part of the Macedonian education system, Milčev modeled—as Fraenkel had done before her—the kind of persistent behavior that is necessary for successful social entrepreneurship. They kept moving forward and eventually found ways to get around the substantial obstacles they had faced.

Fraenkel exhibited this same type of behavior on another front. From his first days in Macedonia, in addition to being concerned about the lack of bilingual education, he was unhappy with the poor quality of TV programming that his daughter Sarah was watching. Although she understood the Macedonian language, the tube offered her mostly not so funny clown shows, as well as subtitled cartoons from the United States and Germany. Along with Sheldon Himelfarb, then executive producer of Common Ground Productions, Fraenkel came to me with a proposal to produce a dramatic children's TV series in Macedonia that promoted ethnic understanding. They had already convinced Children's Television Workshop, the producer of *Sesame Street*, to be their partner.

Although I am too old to have been part of the *Sesame* generation, I recognized that a partnership with *Sesame* would add a huge amount of credibility to Search's then fledging efforts to use TV productions to defuse conflict. I was impressed that Ed Palmer, one of the original developers of *Sesame*, had traveled to Skopje three times to help design the curriculum at the heart of the series. Even so, I was not at all enthusiastic about making a children's series. I thought we should concentrate on adults who, from my perspective, were the ones threatening ethnic violence. That turned out to be a short-sighted view on my part. To his credit, Fraenkel did not give up. He had a vision that TV drama could shift the attitudes and behaviors of future generations of Macedonians—and it did. But that would be years away.

When Fraenkel first proposed the series to me, I told him that dramatic television programming for children was a lovely idea, but I was not convinced that we could find the money to produce it. However, I did not categorically veto the idea, and I held out a glimmer of hope by reminding him that Search had a policy that if staff members recommended a new project that was consistent with our vision—which this project clearly was—and if funding could be found to implement it, I would approve it. Thus, I gave him a green light but I felt it was really a yellow light because I didn't think the money would be there. It turned out that I was wrong, and my lack of enthusiasm was misguided.

It took Fraenkel many months to find the $1.5 million needed to produce the first eight episodes of the series that was to be named *Nashe Maalo* (Our

Neighborhood). Among many potential funders, Fraenkel had approached the U.S. Agency for International Development (USAID). Unfortunately, its director for Macedonia had not seemed interested. But Fraenkel found a work-around. At a reception, he approached Christopher Hill, the U.S. ambassador to Macedonia and described the children's TV series he had in mind. In making his pitch, Fraenkel was able to drop the name of our prospective partner, *Sesame Street*, which represented the gold standard in children's television. The ambassador responded to the proposal with enthusiasm. He said that such a series was likely to have a greater impact on Macedonia than most of the foreign aid projects that were then being carried out. He assured Fraenkel that he would push USAID to provide a substantial part of the $1.5 million needed.

Even though a U.S. ambassador such as Chris Hill was the nominal boss of the USAID director, what Fraenkel did in going around the USAID chain of command was risky. Often when a U.S. ambassador told USAID to fund a project—and I learned this the hard way from personal experience—the USAID staff would become resentful that the ambassador was interfering on their turf, and they would either find myriad reasons not to do what he or she wanted or would slow-walk the project and wait for the ambassador to go home. However, Fraenkel figured he had nothing to lose, and in this case he picked the right person to intervene because Hill was a very forceful ambassador. Due to Hill's urging, USAID agreed to provide about $500,000 to get the project rolling. With this pledge of support in hand, Fraenkel was able to find sufficient funding for the TV series not only to pay for the first season but for four additional seasons. In the end, donors included the British, Dutch, Swedish, and Swiss governments, as well as the John D. and Catherine T. MacArthur, Skoll, and C. S. Mott foundations.

The last obstacle came unexpectedly in 1998 when war broke out in neighboring Kosovo, and thousands of Kosovar Albanians fled into Macedonia—much to the unhappiness of most Macedonians. Previously, Macedonian state television (called MTV) had agreed to provide production facilities and to broadcast *Nashe Maalo*. However, with bombs falling across the border in Kosovo and a refugee crisis emerging, MTV decided it did not want to air a series that involved ethnic tolerance. Obviously, an unforeseen event like the war in Kosovo could have been a disaster for us, but we did not give up. We managed to construct our own sound-stage in an empty warehouse and cobbled together a network of independent TV stations that reached the whole country. However, in those days computer-based transmission was not yet possible, and we had to rely on the mail and motorcycle couriers to deliver broadcast tapes to local stations. Altogether forty-one episodes of *Nashe Maalo* were aired, and it was a huge hit. Even MTV came around. Four years after it had refused to broadcast the series, it agreed to show it in both the Slavic Macedonian and Albanian languages.

Civilization: The Magazine of the Library of Congress wrote this about *Nashe Maalo*: "Don't expect a Balkan Big Bird or cuddly Muppets. Think subtitles and a rap theme in four languages."

The series centered on an apartment house in which four families lived—one Slavic Macedonian, one Albanian, one Turkish, and one Roma (Gypsy). At the suggestion of *Sesame*, we made the apartment house into an animated, talking character named Karmen (figure 5.3). Only the kids could hear Karmen's wise and witty words, and she became an electronic version of the Delphic Oracle. She appeared on the screen of an old TV set, and she used magic to fill the kids' heads with visions of what might be possible. In the process, she helped the children understand the fears and

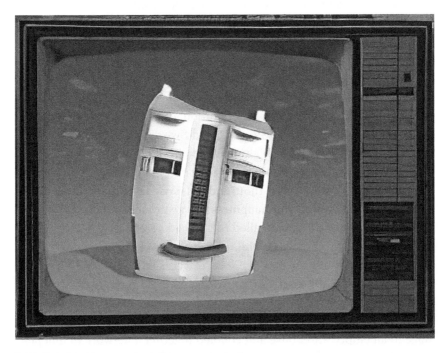

FIGURE 5.3 Karmen, the talking apartment house.

beliefs that led to ethnic prejudice, and she showed the kids how they could put themselves into the shoes of others.

One program featured a story about a Turkish girl who, without asking permission, borrowed her mom's necklace. When the mother realized that the necklace was missing, she immediately assumed that it had been stolen by the Roma woman who worked for the family as a cleaning lady. In the end, the daughter admitted that she was the guilty party, and the mother realized that blaming the cleaner without evidence was a result of her stereotyping of the Roma.

In producing *Nashe Maalo*, we learned a great deal from our *Sesame* partners (figure 5.4). For many years, they had made programs "based on the belief that television can help children learn." *Nashe Maalo* combined *Sesame*'s curriculum-based approach with what was then our six years of experience in conflict prevention in Macedonia. The intended outcome was to break down ethnic stereotypes and promote understanding. The series was based on extensive research and analysis, involving both before-and-after studies and focus groups. It spun off a number-one music video, a magazine, a teacher's guide, and even a puppet theater.

FIGURE 5.4 Mozaik kids *Nashe Maalo* cast members.

Our colleagues from *Sesame* impressed upon us how important it was to conduct thorough evaluations to confirm that the series was achieving its goals. Independent evaluators found that before watching the series only 30 percent of Macedonian children were willing to invite a kid from another ethnic group to their home to play, but the percentage doubled to 60 percent among kids who viewed the first eight episodes of *Nashe Maalo*. We felt hugely validated by this extraordinary attitude shift that the series created just in its first year.

In 2004 when the series came to an end, we commissioned evaluators to poll 1,200 Macedonian kids to provide a final look at what we had accomplished. Here are the key findings:

• 91 percent of Macedonia's kids watched the series, as did 75 percent of the country's adults.
• 32 percent of the children discussed the series in school with their teachers.
• Almost all viewers came to understand what was known in Macedonia as the *Nashe Maalo logic*, which involved "a more open attitude of inclusivity (embracing diversity), pioneered by the show. . . . It provided a national reference point because of its impact as a model."

Although we were gratified by what we accomplished with *Nashe Maalo*, we understood that a single TV series, however popular, could not overcome the root causes of interethnic mistrust and hostility. But it could help considerably, and we did something that had never been accomplished before in Macedonia: We created a model of ethnic tolerance—"a national reference point"—that most citizens, regardless of ethnicity, came to recognize as the ideal, even when they did not live up to it.

In 2001, when armed conflict broke out inside Macedonia, A1 TV in Skopje asked our permission, which we readily granted, to rerun *Nashe Maalo* episodes on a daily basis. In addition, cast members filmed a public statement in their native languages with the theme, "We want our neighborhood to be a peaceful neighborhood." And the child actors, who had appeared in the series and had become national matinee idols, made six public service announcements (PSAs) to tamp down the violence. Refet Abazi, one of the series directors, described the impact of the series as follows:

You know how in the U.S. you have adults who identify as being of the *Sesame* generation? Well, here in Macedonia, you have created the *Nashe Maalo* generation.

Nashe Maalo was appreciated at Macedonia's highest level. Boris Trajkovski, who was Kiro Gligorov's successor as president of the country, had this to say about the series: "Knowing the positive outcome of Search for Common Ground in Macedonia's previous activities, the government hopes that *Nashe Maalo* will become an integral part of kids' everyday life, not only in this but also in future generations."

President Trajkovski also said the Mozaik kindergartens are "imperative for our country." Like President Gligorov before him, Trajkovski was clearly an enthusiastic supporter of our work. Perhaps in some places having the backing of the president of the country may not be a good idea. Nevertheless, having started with Robert Frowick, the Lafayette of Macedonia, we had built a network of credible supporters across the country who helped us immensely in preventing the kind of ethnic warfare that was so disastrously waged in other parts of the Balkans.

6

Expect the Dunbar Factor

Peter was blind, and a seeing-eye dog named Dunbar went everywhere with him. In 1998, Peter applied for a job with Search in Washington, D.C. We had never employed a person who could not see and who needed a guide dog. Peter was clearly qualified, but I felt compelled to ask him a whole set of questions that I would not have asked a seeing person. Would he be able to use our computer system? How many times a day would Dunbar have to be walked? Would Dunbar foul the office if Peter was too busy to take him out? Peter had no problem providing satisfactory answers. I offered him the job, and he accepted.

There was one important question that I did not think to ask: Was anyone in our office allergic to dogs? The question simply did not occur to me because I was a dog lover. I soon was told that I did have a colleague with a canine allergy. It was Angela, my assistant, and I certainly did not want to lose her. What to do? We needed a work-around. We moved Peter into a large office with plenty of space for Dunbar to lie on the floor while Peter worked. This office was located as far away as possible from Angela's, which was next to mine. Whenever Peter needed to attend a meeting with me, I went to his office. Usually staff members came to me for meetings, but Peter and Dunbar were granted ongoing exceptions. Thus Angela was able to maintain her distance from Dunbar.

I learned a specific lesson and a very general one from this experience. Specifically, before hiring someone with a service dog, find out if any colleagues might have an allergy. More important was the general lesson: Even when social entrepreneurs ask all the questions they think are relevant, important issues may arise that should have been considered but weren't because the entrepreneurs didn't know what they didn't know. In pursuing their goals, social entrepreneurs are likely to face unanticipated, often destabilizing events. Even the best laid plans and the most thorough research will not prevent these from occurring. The only defense is to realize, in the words of former Secretary of Defense Donald Rumsfeld, that there are going to be "unknown unknowns." I call this the *Dunbar Factor*. Principle #6 of social entrepreneurship is "expect the Dunbar Factor." There is no escape from this. In response, social entrepreneurs need to be agile enough to minimize the damage and to make the most out of unforeseen events. To put it another way, if you have a lemon, make lemonade.

In my experience, the Dunbar Factor most often comes into play when social entrepreneurs are launching new ventures. For example, in chapter 5 I described how unexpected warfare broke out in Kosovo just as our Macedonian program was about to begin production of the *Nashe Maalo* television series. It had not occurred to our staff that this might happen, that it would result in a massive flow of Kosovar refugees fleeing into Macedonia, and that a by-product would be that Macedonian TV would renege on its agreement to broadcast our series. Since we had not foreseen this possibility, we had no contingency plan for dealing with it. Nevertheless, we were sufficiently nimble to patch together a work-around, but things certainly would have been easier if we had asked the right questions in advance and had come up earlier with a Plan B.

For us at Search, the central African country of Burundi provided numerous examples of the Dunbar Factor. Our involvement there grew out of an unexpected challenge. In October 1994, my old friend Lionel Rosenblatt invited me to a meeting where the growing violence in Burundi was to be discussed. Rosenblatt and I had dated roommates in college, and we had served together as civilian advisors in Vietnam. After a successful diplomatic career in which he had specialized in saving countless lives of people fleeing violent conflict, Rosenblatt had retired from the Foreign Service and become head of Refugees International, an NGO that protected displaced people around the world. When he asked me to come to this meeting, it was only a few months after genocide had taken place in Rwanda, and he feared that Burundi, which bordered Rwanda and had a similar mix of Hutus and Tutsis, was headed down a similar path. Although the killing in Burundi had not yet reached the horrendous level that had occurred in Rwanda, massacres had become regular occurrences, and thousands of Burundians were dying every month in interethnic carnage. One of Rosenblatt's main concerns was that clandestine radio stations in Burundi were broadcasting hateful programming that mirrored the content of Rwanda's *Radio des Milles Collines.* This Hutu-run station had incited mass murder with inflammatory programming that had described Tutsis as cockroaches and exhorted listeners to stamp them out.

Rosenblatt knew that Search was involved in media programming, and he wanted us to use jamming to stop *hate radio* in Burundi. I explained to him that we had no experience with jamming. Instead I said that our specialty was to produce programs that brought people together and lessened violence. Rosenblatt replied, "You claim to be an organization that prevents conflict. If you can't do something to stop Burundi from becoming a killing field, what good are you?"

Rosenblatt's words stung deeply. I was strongly committed to preventive action, and I felt the need to act, as Susan did when I told her about the conversation. On the spot, she and I decided to travel to Burundi to explore what an organization like ours could do. We invited Rosenblatt to join us, and he accepted.

Despite our decision to fly off, we had a problem to overcome. Search didn't have the money to pay for the trip. At this point in our history, we had virtually no funds on hand to develop new projects. However, I knew a donor who liked to provide seed money for innovative ventures. This was John Whitehead, a former deputy secretary of state and a Goldman Sachs banker. I contacted him, and his foundation sent a check for $10,000 in return mail.

Within a week, Rosenblatt, Susan, and I were on a plane headed to Bujumbura, Burundi's capital, to see what we could do to help defuse the violence. Before leaving, we sought recommendations on people to meet. The key referral came from Kofi Annan, who was then the UN's Under-Secretary-General for Peacekeeping. He recommended that we contact Ambassador Ahmedou Ould-Abdallah, the Special Representative in Burundi of the UN Secretary-General. This turned out to be particularly important because, as we learned later, Ould-Abdallah was the unofficial leader of the international community's effort to prevent genocide. He also proved to be a common grounder to his core. (Years later, after he retired, he would become a Search board member.)

When we contacted Ould-Abdallah's office to set up an appointment, we were told that he was scheduled to be in Europe during the week we were going to be in Burundi. Fortunately we were able to arrange a meeting with him in a restaurant in Brussels, where we had a long layover between planes. Over lunch, we made our introductions. Then I launched into a description of how Search might contribute to reducing the level of violence in Burundi. To illustrate I started to draw a diagram on what I thought was a paper napkin; however, the napkin turned out to be made of linen. Susan quickly realized that my pen was ruining the fabric, and she told me to stop. Somewhat embarrassed, I continued my pitch with words only. Unbeknownst to me, Susan stuck the defaced napkin in her purse. Months later she put it into a picture frame with a caption below it that said this was my "conceptual framework" for Burundi and presented it to me (figure 6.1).

In my view, the drawing, which remained on my office wall for the next twenty years, turned out to be a graphic representation of all the questions I didn't know enough to ask when I first went to Burundi. In other words, it was a picture of the *not-knowing* quality that is inherent in the Dunbar Factor.

For whatever reason, Ould-Abdallah did not disqualify us—neither because I had ruined the napkin nor because we at Search had little prior knowledge about Burundi. Perhaps he was desperate; perhaps no other NGO had approached him and claimed that it could help prevent violence; perhaps he was impressed by our experience elsewhere and our tentative plans for Burundi; or perhaps he was persuaded by our passion and commitment. It was probably a combination of all of the above. In any case, he encouraged us to begin activities in Burundi as soon as possible.

At that point, we still did not have any funding to set up a program, and Ould-Abdallah became our champion. He proceeded to call the USAID country director and urged that we should be given an emergency grant. As a direct result, USAID came through in what seemed to be record time. Two months after we first met Ould-Abdallah, we opened an office in Bujumbura.

With Ould-Abdallah's agreement, we decided that our first activity would be to create a radio studio that would produce programming to counter hate radio. Radio was the only medium that reached the whole country,

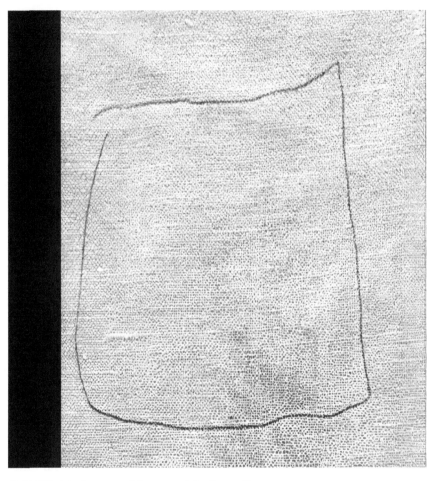

FIGURE 6.1 Conceptual framework for Burundi.

and its impact—albeit negative—had been demonstrated in Rwanda. In Burundi we wanted to produce programming that had the opposite effect—i.e., that encouraged peaceful coexistence, spurred dialogue, and reduced polarization. We believed that the antidote to hate radio was neither jamming nor love radio. In our view, what was needed was *common ground radio*.

To this end, we established Studio *Ijambo* ("wise words" in Kirundi, the language spoken by both Hutus and Tutsis). By setting up a radio studio as opposed to a station, we reasoned that we would be less vulnerable to closure by the authorities if programming angered them; that we could avoid the hassle of obtaining a broadcast license and finding transmitters; and that we would not be competing with the country's other stations. Instead we would be supporting those stations by furnishing them with high-quality programming, which we would provide at no cost. By being cooperative and generous, we would be following our organizational practice of modeling the behavior we wanted to encourage in the population as a whole.

Studio *Ijambo* hired both Hutu and Tutsi reporters, and it became Burundi's only media producer with people of both ethnicities working together on an equal basis. We asked them to leave their ethnicity at the door. To be employed by the studio, staff members needed to be committed not to the predominance of their ethnic group but to the promotion of independent, accurate journalism. This was not easy. As Bryan Rich, the studio's first director, explained, "In Burundi, being 'independent' is equated with betrayal, and therefore the notion of independence itself is alien and dangerous."

Despite the death of one of our reporters in what was generally believed to be an ethnically instigated murder, Studio *Ijambo* became hugely popular and reached a mass audience in both the Tutsi and Hutu communities. During our peak years, we produced fifteen hours a week of original programming. When the government forbade any contact with rebel groups, we spliced together parallel interviews that allowed the parties to hear each other's perspectives. We convened roundtable discussions with people who had been unwilling to talk directly to each other. The studio even had a fleet of motorcycles enabling our journalists to travel to remote parts of the country and phone in news reports.

The studio produced a considerable amount of investigative reporting that relied on mixed Hutu-Tutsi teams of reporters who provided protection for each other during dangerous assignments. At one point in 1998, the studio broke a story about a massacre committed by government soldiers who were mostly Tutsis. Several high government officials wanted to penalize the studio for uncovering this atrocity, but the country's president, Pierre Buyoya, himself a Tutsi, disagreed. He said that our reporters were only doing their jobs. As a result, Burundi experienced a major turnaround. A few days after our report aired, the government set up a commission of inquiry and arrested three officers involved in the killings. Never before had there been accountability for human rights abuses; impunity had long been the norm. Afterward, the UN Security Council took special note of this positive change.

In addition to investigative reports, the studio produced numerous multi-episodic radio series that became national institutions. One that was particularly popular was called *Pillars of Humanity*; it told real-life stories of Hutus who had saved the lives of Tutsis and of Tutsis who had saved Hutus. The idea was to portray these people as heroes and, in the process, to redefine the meaning of heroism to illustrate that common humanity transcended ethnic loyalties. Each episode ended with a call-in segment during which listeners were encouraged to tell their own stories of cross-ethnic life-saving. When we launched the series, our staff members estimated they would only be able to find enough material for about ten episodes. They had no idea that the programs would unleash a flood of accounts from all over the country and that this outpouring would keep the weekly series on the air for six years.

A typical episode featured the story of individual heroes—for example, Rebecca, a Tutsi who fended off armed men and saved forty-one Hutus, said:

> I did not protect them because I am a Tutsi or a Hutu. . . . We should not put forward our own ethnic group, but rather our humanity. We are created by the same God. We are the same people.

Another episode focused on Fulgence, a pupil in a school that was attacked by militants who, like him, were Hutus. The attackers demanded that the students separate into two groups, one of Tutsis and the other of Hutus. The students realized that that those who were identified as Tutsis would be killed, and they all refused to reveal their ethnicity. Even after the attackers started to hack the students with machetes and shoot them, the students would not relent. In all, forty-two young people of both ethnicities died. Fulgence was one of three survivors. "My ethnic group is the human race," he said. "We stayed together to the end."

In 2004 the *Pillars of Humanity* series finally ended. Then, under the leadership of Lena Slachmuijlder, the studio's director at the time, we sponsored a *Heroes Summit* to honor and showcase people like Rebecca and Fulgence. The *Summit* was successful beyond expectations. Internationally, ninety news articles appeared, along with many radio and TV pieces. A high school teacher in St. Louis, Missouri, contacted us to say he planned to integrate material from the *Summit* into his World Religions class. We received a note from a woman involved with recognizing

Righteous Gentiles who had saved the lives of Jews during World War II. She wrote, "Thank you for your inspiration. You reminded me of our common humanity and of the need to stop genocide wherever it happens."

A Burundian high school principal wrote, "The *Summit* has had an immeasurable impact. The world is full of people famous for their bad deeds. There are others who act with their heart and faith, but we hardly know them. What Studio *Ijambo* has done is to take these numerous heroes from the shadows and present them in front of the nation as the genuine flames of peace and reconciliation for Burundi." As Roger Conrad, a senior USAID official, noted, "You have introduced the vocabulary of peace and reconciliation to the national conversation at all levels, where previously only words of hate and mistrust were heard."

The *Pillars of Humanity* series used a documentary format. In addition, we produced fictional drama, which we referred to as *soap opera for social change* (figure 6.2). As a boy, I had listened avidly to radio soaps—my favorites were *The Lone Ranger* and *The Shadow*. By the time we worked in Burundi, radio drama had mostly disappeared in the West, but I felt it would work well in Burundi where radio remained the predominant medium. Our goal was to use good storytelling to reach a mass audience with messages that rose above hatred. We commissioned a well-known Burundian author, Louise Sebazuri, to write scripts for a series called *Our Neighbors, Ourselves.* For six years, the studio produced two shows a week, completing 616 episodes that were broadcast on national radio. Surveys found that the series was heard by 87 percent of the population. Plotlines focused on two families, one Hutu and the other Tutsi (although we never said which was which). They lived next to each other, and the two mothers struggled to maintain a cooperative relationship and protect their children from the devastation of violence. A front-page *Wall Street Journal* article stated that the series was designed "to show that it is possible to overcome the mistrust that prevails between the minority Tutsi and majority Hutu groups."

At one point, for technical reasons, Burundi national radio failed to broadcast a new episode. Soon armed soldiers appeared at Studio *Ijambo*. Our staff members were understandably frightened. But the soldiers said they had come in peace and wanted only to obtain a tape of the missing show. They feared that the troops might mutiny if they could not listen to the latest episode. Needless to say, our staff gladly provided a copy.

Although we made no claim that *common ground radio*—in Burundi or anywhere—had the power for good that its hate-filled opposite had for

FIGURE 6.2 Recording a radio soap opera segment.

evil, we believed that, over time, positive programming had a substantial impact in defusing conflict. A poll conducted for USAID found that 82 percent of Burundians thought that Studio *Ijambo* greatly encouraged reconciliation. The programming kept alive, in a very difficult environment, the idea that there were real alternatives to violence. Indeed, ABC *Nightline's* Ted Koppel called Studio *Ijambo* "the voice of hope in Burundi."

After the studio had been operating for almost two years, another unforeseen event occurred that exemplified the Dunbar Factor. None of our staff had ever thought to ask what we would do if a coup d'état took place, but that is exactly what happened in 1996 when Burundi's military overthrew the country's Hutu president and replaced him with a Tutsi.

In addition to being appalled by the coup, we were shaken to learn that it put at risk our whole program in Burundi. At that time, USAID was still our sole funder, and we had no choice but to comply with its directives.

That put us in a vulnerable position, and we had not considered all of the implications. Our overriding concern had been to prevent bloodshed, and we had been glad to take support from the U.S. government to accomplish this end. However, the coup triggered the provision in U.S. law stating that whenever a military takeover occurs USAID must suspend most of its funding. After the coup, USAID notified us that we should shut down. We felt that this was exactly the wrong time to end our programming. After all, the coup and the ongoing violence were rooted in ethnic conflict that we were working to defuse. We were convinced that we were needed more now than ever.

We had to find some sort of work-around that would allow us to stay open. Otherwise, we felt we were likely to lose most of what we had accomplished. I quickly made a *Hail Mary* move. I sent a letter directly to Brian Atwood, the overall head of USAID in Washington, D.C. I asked for a waiver that would allow us to continue our programs. My request bypassed at least four layers of USAID bureaucracy. I figured that we had nothing to lose, and Brian was an old friend with whom I had worked closely in my days as a Senate aide. My appeal apparently hit the mark. Shortly thereafter we received a waiver that meant we did not have to close.

Not only could we keep operating, but there was an unforeseen result, which from our organizational perspective was highly positive. No longer did we have to share the USAID budget with numerous other NGOs that had been receiving USAID funds. After the coup, USAID was supporting only Search and one other organization. As a result, we soon were receiving a much larger share of the USAID budget than ever before. Although the total amount of our grants never amounted to more than $3 million a year, the funds we received enabled us to greatly increase the scope of our activities. For the first time, we had the means to work across an entire country and to carry out what we called *societal conflict prevention*. Obviously, it helped that Burundi was comparatively small—about the same size as Maryland.

As we expanded, our activities stayed rooted in the simple idea that undergirded our work from the beginning: *Understand the differences and act on the commonalities.* Within that framework, we built a diverse toolbox that included traditional conflict resolution techniques such as mediation, facilitation, and training, along with less conventional ones involving media production, music, dance, sport, and community organizing.

One of our more innovative tools was what we called *domestic shuttle diplomacy.* Henry Kissinger had pioneered shuttle diplomacy by flying from one Middle East capital to another. To play a similar mediating role—but without using an airplane—we brought in Jan van Eck, a former ANC Member of the South African Parliament. Susan had worked closely with him in the South African peace process, and she had great confidence in him. In Burundi, van Eck operated outside official structures to promote dialogue and solve problems among leaders of conflicting factions. For his first two years, we used our USAID grant to pay his salary. While we found van Eck to be highly effective, he was too independent a soul for the U.S. government, and at a certain point we were told we could no longer keep him on the payroll. Since we had no other source of funds, we had no way to provide for him. However, van Eck was not deterred, and he remained committed to working for peace in Burundi. For the next ten years, he somehow managed to find sufficient funds—including his own personal money—to spend about half his time in the country. Van Eck's key to success was persistence. He kept showing up, and he was generally regarded as a trusted intermediary who maintained contact with virtually every party to the conflict, including rebel leaders with whom almost no one else was talking. He brokered many agreements—small and large—and we continued to informally support his efforts. Here is what a USAID-sponsored evaluation—carried out before we were ordered to fire him—had to say about van Eck's work:

> Leaders on all sides of the political (and ethnic) divide credit the project with helping, at a time when the idea of negotiations was unthinkable to either side. . . . One senior participant went so far as to say that "the internal partnership we have today, a thing we couldn't imagine less than two years ago, is the fruit of a tree gently planted and patiently watered by Jan van Eck."

Our societal model called for our staff members to be immersed in local culture. They needed to have a deep sense of where they were. The conflicts in Burundi, as everywhere, were complex, and we recognized that it took deep engagement to understand what was happening and how to take preventive action. Expatriates could have that kind of capacity, as Jan van Eck demonstrated, but we recognized that the people with the deepest understanding were those native to the country. In addition, we also brought in a few expatriates who identified with neither ethnic group. We did not employ people who would only parachute into the country for a short stay. Like Jan van Eck, the internationals needed to be willing to remain in Burundi for long periods of time.

A key part of our societal strategy was the Women's Peace Center. It brought together thousands of Tutsi and Hutu women to promote dialogue and catalyze joint action (figure 6.3). Across Burundi, the center supported about three hundred ethnically mixed women's associations and helped their members rebuild destroyed communities. With violence erupting all over the country, it was one of the few safe havens where women of both ethnicities could meet and deal with shared concerns.

In Burundi, as in so many other countries, women were not seen to be equal to men. In our view, much of the violence was fueled by macho attitudes connected to saving face and seeking revenge. We noted that men did most of the killing, and women were much more open to reconciliation. One of our core ideas was to empower women to be peacemakers. We never went so far as to use the tactic featured in the Greek drama *Lysistrata*—to have the women withhold sex until the men made peace—but that tactic certainly occurred to us and provided a metaphorical backdrop for our work.

FIGURE 6.3 Women's Peace Center solidarity event.

The following account of two extraordinary ladies, Léonie Barakomeza and Yvonne Ryakiye, exemplifies the activities of the Women's Peace Center. These two women were born in the same locality, but they did not know each other. When fighting broke out in 1993 and their communities were destroyed, Barakomeza and her fellow Tutsis fled to one side of a river; Ryakiye and the Hutus went to the other side. In 1996, the two met through the Women's Peace Center, and they began working together. Unlike most of their neighbors, they were willing to cross the river that separated them. Accused of being traitors to their group, they persisted. Other women followed their example, and links grew. They created a women's association and urged everyone to return home. Despite meager means, they pooled resources and built forty brick houses for both Hutu and Tutsi families. Their efforts were recognized, along with eight other Burundian women, when they were nominated for the 2005 Nobel Peace Prize.

Among the targets of our societal approach were young, male militia members who were paid a few dollars a day by political leaders to attack and generally terrorize the other ethnic group. In 1999, we formed a partnership with a Burundian NGO called JAMAA to launch an initiative to reintegrate and rehabilitate young Tutsi and Hutu fighters, mostly child soldiers. We originally called this effort the *Working with Killers* project, but we soon dropped that incendiary name, even though it accurately described what we were doing. The name was not supportive of our goal of helping participants leave behind their bloody pasts and create a better future.

The project represented a stretch for us because we were working directly with young men who had committed horrendous deeds. Why did we deal with these people?—because they were at the heart of the conflict. Our job in Burundi was not to make judgments but to facilitate peacemaking. A key part of our strategy was to give these young men a chance to speak, to compare experiences, and as incredible as it may seem, to build trust. We came to see that Tutsi and Hutu participants were mirror images of each other. Both groups reflected fear, mistrust, and negative stereotypes.

The project started with two Hutus and two Tutsis who had served in opposing militias. These four had all undergone something of a catharsis by telling their stories in a documentary film produced by Bryan Rich, Studio *Ijambo's* first director, and Alexis Sinduhije, one of the studio's original reporters. With our support and that of JAMAA, they invited many of their fellow militiamen to participate in an overnight workshop that brought together thirty-six young men from both sides of the ethnic divide. Participants spent the first evening eating, playing cards, listening to music, and watching a movie on teen violence. As time passed, it became clear that no one wanted to go to bed. The adult facilitators finally decided that they needed to force the issue. There was silence. We had not foreseen that the youth would feel it was foolhardy to sleep in the same building with people they were afraid would murder them. This fear of being physically at risk was completely outside of our experience, and it was another example of the Dunbar Factor. Our staff members had not thought to ask questions about whether the participants would find the sleeping arrangements to be acceptable. They didn't know that they didn't know how to handle the situation. The lesson learned was that whenever we worked with people with blood on their hands particular attention had to be given to convincing participants that they were safe from attack.

Around midnight, a work-around emerged. Assurances from the adults, plus fatigue, won out, and the group agreed to go to bed. In the morning, having survived the night, the young men looked at each other with fresh eyes. First they played soccer, and then they gathered in a circle. For an hour, they spoke in generalities until one of them declared, "This is a joke! We're not here to discuss what we heard happened; we're here to talk about us!" What followed was an animated exchange of shocking stories. Participants described the atrocities in which they had been involved—for example, watching victims die gruesome deaths and seeing family members executed. Being exposed to such atrocities had pushed many of them to seek violent revenge. Nevertheless, the group was able to discover an important point of common ground: namely, both the Tutsi and the Hutu militiamen felt they had been exploited by political leaders who had paid them to be killers.

In the end, participants agreed to organize interethnic soccer matches and to sponsor small-scale economic development projects. This group became the nucleus of our youth activities. We contributed funding, provided platforms for them to express themselves, and explained our suggestions about process. Participants went on to produce a comic book called *Le Meilleur Choix* (The Best Choice) that described the origins of the violence and encouraged other young people not to be manipulated by unscrupulous politicians. The comic books were so compelling that

Burundi's Ministry of Education printed tens of thousands and made the comics part of the curriculum for the country's schools.

This use of comics reached young people in a language that was familiar and accessible to them. It was yet another example of our efforts to speak to our target audience in their own idiom. Because violent conflict in Burundi, as in so many places, depended on mass stereotyping, demonizing, and dehumanizing, we believed that popular culture could play a key part in reversing the process. We recognized that conflict was rarely an intellectual exercise, and we were convinced of the need to reach people on an emotional level. We believed that conflict prevention had to operate on both the head and the heart.

Much of Studio *Ijambo*'s programming reflected this insight. The studio even employed a full-time disc-jockey who produced *music-for-peace* programs. As an added touch, we enlisted the Jamaican Rastafarian reggae star Ziggy Marley, who had a huge following in Burundi, to record PSAs. We also recognized that, above all, in Burundi popular culture involved drumming and dancing. So we organized national drumming competitions and held giant music festivals in Bujumbura.

In sum, societal conflict prevention in Burundi required us to be *weavers*. Our task was to knit together multiple strands to help mend a country that was torn and broken. As an independent evaluator said in a report to USAID, "This entrepreneurial, risk-taking approach should be seen as a model for future interventions in conflict situations."

For us at Search, Burundi was the operational proving ground for societal conflict prevention, and we subsequently adapted the overall concept and many of the specific activities to our work in other countries—in full recognition that each place is different, with its own unique history and culture. In our view, about 50 percent of our toolbox worked in other places, and 50 percent did not—and we never knew in advance which 50 percent was which. For us, the keys were creativity and agility. We were convinced that standardized, off-the-shelf approaches were much less likely to be effective than customized ones, but we almost always found similarities between countries. Everywhere there was a storytelling tradition that we could integrate into our media programming, and everywhere people in conflict saw themselves as victims.

We regarded peace as a process, not an event. It needed to be "patiently watered"—as a Burundian official had put it in describing peace agreements that were brokered by Jan van Eck. Although we appreciated—and yearned for—those wonderful moments when agreements were signed, we recognized that real peace required more than signatures. Even if top leaders were able to reach agreement, for peace to take hold, we believed the majority of people had to want the violence to end. Thus we sought to create an environment across Burundi in which citizens could step back from fear. To counter extremism, we encouraged moderation, and we made maximum use of indigenous wisdom.

As we moved our societal approach into other places, we adapted the methodologies we had put into play in Burundi. We replicated Studio *Ijambo* under the name of *Talking Drum* Studio in Liberia, Sierra Leone, and Guinea. Participatory community theater, which we developed on a small scale in Burundi, became a huge hit in the Democratic Republic of Congo, where our drama troupes used theater to resolve local conflicts in front of audiences that totaled more than two million people. Some Burundian projects, such as national drumming contests, would not have traveled well, and we did not try them elsewhere. But everywhere we worked, we followed the Burundian example of inventing new forms of societal programming that fit with local sensibilities.

Most of the work we did in Burundi took place at the grassroots level, and it can be described as *bottom-up.* At the same time, we recognized the extraordinary importance of *top-down* peacemaking. We came to see that bottom-up and top-down approaches were complementary, and that each was more likely to be successful when the other was present. We believed that our societal work played a key role in creating an environment inside Burundi that was supportive of the official peace negotiations held at Arusha in Tanzania. These talks were led first by Julius Nyerere, the former president of Tanzania. After Nyerere died in 1999, South Africa's Nelson Mandela took over and guided the Burundians to a political settlement, which included national elections and interethnic power sharing.

Unfortunately, neither that agreement nor our bottom-up efforts resolved all of Burundi's problems, and many political leaders refused to abandon their zero-sum approaches. Burundi remains fragile. But compared to 1995 when the country was on the brink of genocide, extraordinary progress has been made. An outside evaluator for USAID summed up our role in the process this way:

These early accomplishments and the well-recognized SFCG call to "leave your ethnicity at the door," combined with the distinction of being one of the few international organizations to stay on in Burundi throughout the crisis, have established SFCG with an extraordinarily high degree of credibility and trust. USAID, and the other program funders, are to be commended for demonstrating the flexibility, responsiveness, and vision to move swiftly and decisively in launching these activities, even in the face of major uncertainties about the shape they were to ultimately take. This entrepreneurial, risk-taking approach should be seen as a model for future interventions in conflict situations.

7

Make Yesable Propositions

Roger Fisher and William Ury wrote about "yesable proposition" in their landmark book *Getting to Yes*. Principle #7 of social entrepreneurship is "make yesable propositions." The concept is not complicated. Indeed, it is so simple I have found that many people brush it off as childish.

A "yesable" proposition is a proposal shaped so that the person to whom it is addressed responds "yes." When people—children or adults—internalize the idea and make it a regular part of their interaction with others, the results can be life-changing. When I first heard of the concept, I had to ask myself frequently if a proposition was yesable. Over time, however, I internalized the practice to the point that it has become second nature to me.

For a proposition to be yesable, it should include the needs and interests not only of the proposer but of the recipient. If the proposition is only acceptable to the proposer, it is likely to be turned down. If it is only OK with the recipient, it probably reflects pandering.

Here is an example on the personal level. My wife strongly dislikes violent films and TV shows. If I suggest that we watch a violence-filled Quentin Tarantino film, she will definitely refuse. If I had overwhelming power, which I don't, or if there were something else that she very much wanted in return from me, she might grudgingly go along. Nevertheless, an agreement based on a power disparity or on a lopsided trade-off is not likely to be sustainable. However, if I put myself into her shoes and recall that she likes historical English drama, I might propose that we watch *The Crown*. To this proposition, she will almost certainly say "yes." Since I also enjoy historical drama, we will have found a *win-win* solution.

The ability to make yesable propositions is useful to everyone. However, it is especially important for social entrepreneurs. To be adept at making such propositions, social entrepreneurs must understand their own needs as well as those of the parties with whom they are dealing. In this way, they can increase the possibility that they will be able to move their activities forward and raise enough money to implement their vision.

Whenever social entrepreneurs apply for funds, it is clearly in their interest to receive a positive reply. The chances that this will happen usually increase if they craft their proposal with substance and language that appeal to the potential donor. It is usually a good idea to include the donor's preferred buzzwords and to cite past successes. Above all, a yesable proposal should fall within the guidelines and interests of the person or institution to which it is addressed. No matter how brilliant the construct or how significant the would-be result, seeking contributions for activities not consistent with a donor's priorities tends to be a fool's errand. For example, an entity that funds activities only inside the United States will almost never support international projects; and a donor who concentrates on public health issues is unlikely to fund voters' rights projects. Philanthropists and investors provide money in accordance with their own priorities—not the social entrepreneur's. One New York foundation supports two—and only two—causes: LGBTQ+ rights and the great apes of Africa. The only possible connection is that both of these issues are of great importance to the person who put up the money in the first place, and that person clearly has disparate interests.

Social entrepreneurs can gain insight into the priorities of possible funders by thoroughly googling them. The idea is to dig deep for information that might provide the background for a prospective request. In addition, social entrepreneurs should try to meet funders and establish personal connections. Admittedly, in a time of pandemics and Zoom encounters, face-to-face sessions are often difficult to arrange, but they are definitely worth the trouble. Some donors simply don't want to give out information. In fact, USAID and the European Union have rules against sharing data beyond what is in their calls for proposals, and they will usually not meet with outside organizations that have already submitted proposals. The best time to talk to them is before they have issued their calls for proposals.

An additional way to learn about a funder is to query other organizations that have previously been supported by that particular donor. I have found that the most productive method for obtaining information from others is to accept the premise that fund-raising—like life—does not have to be a zero-sum game. In other words, to get information, social entrepreneurs should be willing to give information. Not only will sharing possible leads enhance their popularity, but on a practical level being tight-fisted about helping others almost never works well. To put it another way, what goes around tends to come around.

There is another aspect to fund-raising that is completely common-sensical. I call it the *Willie Sutton principle*. Sutton, known as *Slick Willie*, was a famous Brooklyn-based bank robber. After the police captured him, he reportedly gave a press conference during which he was asked why he robbed banks. He said the answer was very simple: "That's where the money is." For social entrepreneurs, the takeaway is that money can only be found where there actually is money and where those possessing it are inclined to donate or invest it.

Making yesable propositions is also important when putting together new projects. Whether launching a campaign or lobbying for change, the ideas being presented need to be sufficiently attractive to the target audience to prompt an affirmative response. Social entrepreneurs should be able to enroll others in their activities and bring well-placed individuals into their orbit. Inviting Middle Easterners to a meeting in Paris in the springtime is a much more likely path for having them accept than asking them to travel in the dead of winter to Helsinki—although I once was successful in enticing Arabs and Israelis to come to the latter city in January.

By necessity, during the first years of Search, I was the entrepreneur-in-chief, and I ran the organization from what might be called the seat of my pants. In 1994, after my new wife Susan joined me, Search had dual entrepreneurs. At that time, we employed about a dozen people, and the organization was growing rapidly in both numbers of staff and the scale of work. One result of this growth was the need for substantial changes in how we operated. No longer were Susan and I able to know everything that was happening across the organization, and the administrative burdens were increasing. Our staff was—rightly—concerned about such things as health benefits, pension plans, and vacation days. We needed to update our financial systems, and we even heard requests for an employees' manual. We were at a point where we needed to answer two key questions: Did we really want to keep growing? Would administrative and financial requirements prevent Susan and me from being free to do the conflict prevention work that we loved?

Susan and I had a long discussion about Search's future—and our own. We concluded that we wanted to be agents of global transformation, and to make a difference on that scale we needed to build a comparatively large organization. Otherwise we did not think we would have the ability to address major conflicts. Armed with this reasoning, we opted for continued expansion despite the administrative obstacles we knew we would face. We vowed to build an organization with sufficient structure to function efficiently, but not with so much bureaucracy that it thwarted creativity and innovation. This was easier said than done.

One upshot of our conversation was the realization that Search would need to employ multiple social entrepreneurs in addition to the two of us. We would require people who were skilled at making yesable propositions that resulted in launching new initiatives and the expansion of existing ones. I discovered that there is a word in business literature for staff members who operate in this manner. They are called *intrapreneurs*. Dictionary.com defines such people as those who are "given freedom and financial support to create new products, services, systems, etc. and [who do] not have to follow the corporation's usual routines or protocols." Intrapreneurship was clearly the quality we were looking for when we hired additional senior staff.

Over the years, we brought in many people who displayed intrapreneurial talents. One person who particularly stood out was Lena Slachmuijlder. She began her Search career as the director of Studio *Ijambo* in Burundi. It was she who conceived and brought to life the Heroes Summit described in chapter 6. In 2005, we transferred her from Burundi to the Democratic Republic of Congo (DRC) to serve as our country director.

Susan had led us into the DRC four years earlier and established our first presence there. This central African country, which was the setting of Joseph Conrad's *Heart of Darkness*, proved to be a very difficult place to work. Its history of colonialism, dictatorship, and war had led to millions of deaths, had devastated the infrastructure, and had a huge negative impact on the social fabric. When Slachmuijlder took over, we were working mainly to support the country's peace process. Because the DRC was split between zones controlled by the government and several rebel groups, we had two offices—one in Kinshasa, the capital, and one in Bukavu, in the wild east. Slachmuijlder turned out to be particularly good at making yesable propositions for funding. On her watch, we were able to open five additional offices around the DRC; our staff grew to one hundred people; the budget quintupled to $5.2 million a year; and the program became our largest anywhere in the world. Thus we were able to implement a societal approach despite the vastness of the DRC, which is about the size of the United States east of the Mississippi.

Slachmuijlder's work demonstrated how prolonged engagement and showing up were such important qualities in social entrepreneurship—and social intrapreneurship. However, all good things had to end, and in 2011, after six years in the DRC, she decided that she wanted a change. We did not want to lose her, so we made her an offer she did not refuse. She accepted a new position as Search's chief programming officer based in Washington, D.C., and she became a member of our senior management team. Just before she left the DRC to take on these new duties, she invited me to come and view firsthand what she had accomplished. As a result, I made my first visit ever inside the DRC. (I had once before made an hour's stop in the Kinshasa airport.) I knew comparatively little about what she had been doing because she reported to our Africa director, not to me, and my focus was on the Middle East. But I was curious about her activities, so I put aside a week to visit her and said that I wanted to see as much as I possibly could. She obliged and arranged a full schedule. In essence, she took me on a trip through her *greatest hits*.

My visit started when I walked across the border from Burundi into the eastern DRC, and Slachmuijlder met me. Our first stop was in the nearby town of Uvira, where we visited the Search office. I had never before even heard of Uvira, and I had no idea we even had an office there. I tried to act knowledgeable while our office director, whom I had never met before, briefed me on the work we were doing to strengthen local government and aid the return of refugees.

From Uvira, we drove on an awful road to Lemera, an isolated village where Swedish missionaries had once preached and had left behind church buildings that seemed out of place among the green hills of Africa. Local officials showed us the community radio station, one of eighty-five of our partner stations for which we at Search were producing twenty-two hours of original programming each week. As in Burundi, we operated production studios, not stations. Internet transmission was not yet possible, so CDs of our programs were distributed by plane, bus, and motorcycle to stations around the country. Although in Burundi we had only one production studio, in the much larger DRC we had four, and we made programs in French and four tribal languages.

One of our most popular radio series showcased a fictional, villainous Army officer named Commandant Janvier (figure 7.1). The series revolved around our conviction that we could use popular culture to limit the widespread abuses that were regularly committed by the Congolese Army. As a character, Commandant Janvier embodied how a military man should *not* act. The series lasted for ten years and consisted of hundreds of weekly

FIGURE 7.1 The fictional Army officer Commandant Janvier.

episodes. We increased its impact by widely distributing hundreds of thousands of comic books that depicted the Commandant's (mis)adventures. In the process, the Commandant became the national archetype for a loathsome military man. As one of our scriptwriters said, "If you wanted to let someone know that he was doing something wrong, you just called him a Commandant Janvier."

In Lemera, I watched a participatory theater performance in the village square. It was staged by one of our Search theater troupes, and it was obviously scheduled for my benefit. However, it did not represent a one-off, Potemkin Village-type event because participatory theater was one of our signature techniques. Slachmuijlder and a group of Congolese artists had developed the form when they had combined our common ground approach with Brazilian street theater techniques. They trained scores of actors and actresses who put on thousands of shows that were viewed by more than two million Congolese. The methodology was so effective in resolving local conflicts that we expanded its use to Search programs in several other countries.

The secret ingredient for these performances was to have the actors create a new storyline for each locality. They did this by arriving several hours early in the village where they were scheduled to perform. Then they walked around, listened to conversations, probed the villagers about the conflicts that were dividing the community, and improvised a play that dramatized the key conflicts. Next they restarted the play, paused after each scene, and asked audience members how the characters might have been more successful in dealing with the conflict. Finally, the performers invited audience members to replace them and to act out better ways of resolving the conflict.

After the performance in Lemera, I rode in a van with the actors and actresses on the road to Bukavu. As we rattled along, they shared their individual stories. One was a former child soldier who described the immense pain he had experienced when he had witnessed his parents being dragged away and murdered by a rebel militia group. He said he had wanted to die. However, by joining Search, he eventually found his calling. "I saw I wasn't the only one," he discovered. "I wanted to give the peace I had found to others."

The next morning in Bukavu, I was taken to the Congolese Army's regional headquarters, where I watched a session to *sensitize* a battalion of soldiers on the need for better behavior. This also was not an isolated event staged on my behalf. Search was carrying out thousands of similar sessions, which were facilitated by military men we had trained. These sessions invariably opened up discussions about shame, trauma, and vulnerability. They often ignited a desire to change among participants. The goal was to improve the conduct of soldiers who, deplorably, were among the DRC's prime perpetrators of human rights abuses, particularly sexual violence against women. The DRC had become known as the rape capital of the world, and huge numbers of women and girls had been violated. Many, if not most, Congolese soldiers acted from the mistaken belief that females were a rightful part of war plunder.

Under Slachmuijlder's leadership, we were seeking to instill in the poorly paid and poorly trained military the need to protect civilians—not to harm them. In partnership with ECC-MERU, a Protestant church-based NGO, we worked directly with the Army's Civic and Patriotic Education Service, whose mission included taking care of the well-being of soldiers. The head of this service was General Mulubi Bin Muhemedi, a decent man who was committed to eliminating abusive behavior in the ranks. Unfortunately, before the general started working with us, he had almost no resources to carry out constructive programming.

Together, Slachmuijlder and the general designed a program that sought to retrain the Congolese military and that later was extended to the National Police (figure 7.2). It was called *Tomorrow Is a New Day*, and it was a decentralized effort that followed the army's hierarchical lines. Each battalion or brigade formed a steering committee of senior officers, chaplains, and liaison officers. With initial funding from the UN High Commission for Refugees and subsequently from the Dutch government, we launched twenty steering committees and a full retraining effort in two provinces in the eastern DRC.

In both places, the initiative featured a full toolbox of methodologies that included sensitization training, radio and video programs, participatory theater, and instructional comic books. We also sponsored *solidarity* activities that brought together soldiers and civilians to carry out good works such as cleanups, repairs, harvesting, and sporting events. The idea was to demonstrate to the civilian population that the army could be a positive force in their communities.

Whenever possible, we included soldiers' wives in the training programs. Many wives suffered from both spousal abuse and the stigma of being married to military men, whom the general population often held in low esteem because so many soldiers displayed the kind of abhorrent behavior

FIGURE 7.2 Lena Slachmulder and General Mulubi stand among a class of Congolese army trainees.

embodied on the radio by Commandant Janvier. Virtually no wives supported their husbands being rapists, and the husbands were more likely to realize the error of their ways when their wives were present. One wife commented that our retraining program "was a blessing for every soldier and every soldier's wife. I've seen my husband Henri change. He brings the guidance into our home and shares it with his wife." Added her husband, "When my wife noticed I changed, she fell in love with me again."

After the *Tomorrow Is a New Day* program had been going for about two years, we commissioned comprehensive evaluations in the two provinces where the program had been used. We wanted to know if we were on the right track. The evaluators found 92 percent of the local population judged that abuses had been significantly reduced, and 89 percent believed that due to joint military-civilian activities there had been a marked decrease in forced labor, theft, illegal arrest, extortion, and rape. Here are some quotes from local civilians who were asked what they thought of our retraining efforts:

- If President Kabila wants peace, he should leave the military deployed here in Bunyakiri. We are no longer afraid when we see a military uniform.

- If these military leave our area, we will follow them. Then we know we'll be safe.
- Before, the civilians used to be able to manipulate the Military Police to do bad things. But now they are disciplined and don't allow themselves to be used.

With those evaluations in hand, Slachmuijlder was able to convince more funders to support expansion across the country, and *Tomorrow Is a New Day* became a societal initiative. It eventually reached the entire army, and more than 100,000 soldiers were retrained.

Years later, I asked Slachmuijlder how she was able to get buy-in from General Mulubi and the DRC military leadership. When she began, she said, the Congolese Army was regularly condemned because of the predatory and violent behavior of the troops. Faced with a steady stream of criticism, the army usually reacted with defensiveness and denial. To her credit, Slachmuijlder recognized that there were people inside and outside the ranks who wanted things to change, and she made a decision to work with the army—not to accuse it—even if a large number of soldiers were guilty of horrible abuses.

Regarding General Mulubi, Slachmuijlder said:

I was able to show him empathy. I listened a lot to his story. I understood that he had a very hard job, but I also caught a glimpse of what he wished for. I didn't need to denounce the soldiers—nor would that have helped. . . . I said that I understood the challenges he was facing, and I thought that we could help him achieve his aims. I wanted him to feel safe and to understand that positive change could happen under his leadership.

Yesable propositions were a critical part of making change. It was essential to understand people's needs and not just to try to get them to do what your project proposal said they should do. When you did this, you realized that not everything was about material needs; and that there were also other needs like reputation, appreciation, connection, and trust. Many people thought change would occur in accordance with log-frames.[1] In my view, providing incentives was the key to change. It was our role to design a program that let those incentives drive our work.

---

1. A log-frame is the short name for a logical framework, a planning tool consisting of a matrix that provides an overview of a project's goals, activities, and anticipated results. Donors are concerned with metrics, and they usually require detailed log-frames.

Because *Tomorrow Is a New Day* contained incentives for key players, it was yesable to both the Congolese military and the international community. For General Mulubi, the program provided sufficient resources to make him relevant and to stop conduct of soldiers that he found repugnant. For the army's general staff, which needed to give its approval, the program deflected international criticism and increased the professionalism of the troops. For Western governments that provided funding and needed to show their parliaments that they were not wasting taxpayers' money, the program produced quantifiable results that were verified by independent evaluators. For the soldiers who became the trainers and facilitators of the sensitization sessions, the program allowed them to do the right thing and to gain a certain degree of status. In addition, they earned pocket money, occasional fuel for motorcycles, and a modest amount of office supplies. For the soldiers in the field, in addition to being instructed in international standards of conduct, the program furnished small but tangible inducements, such as time off from normal duties and large quantities of Fanta orange soda—a delicacy in Congolese terms that was regularly served at *sensitization* sessions.

To understand the impact that *Tomorrow Is a New Day* has had, please consider what happened with the Congolese Army's 811th Brigade. Before entering our retraining program, the 811th had an appalling record of theft, rape, and murder. Then the brigade went through thirty-six sensitization sessions that involved 1,026 soldiers, and forty-six officers who were instructed in the need to end impunity for human rights violations. In March 2013, the retrained 811th was deployed to the Katanga region. It was encamped at the Lubumbashi airport when a rebel *Mai Mai* militia attacked the city. The brigade was ordered to counterattack. For the first time in its history, the brigade carried out an armed operation without committing abuses. "We had the option of exterminating them," said Colonel Prince, the commander. "It could have been done within two hours—but given our recent background in human rights and international humanitarian law, we proceeded differently. This is why we systematically encircled them and summoned them to surrender. We are not a terror arm anymore." Added Anne Mutong, a Katangan civil society leader, "This time, I am proud of those soldiers that saved the city without any major collateral damage. They acted like professionals, and they really protected the population."

From Bukavu, the next stop for Slachmuijlder and me was Goma, sixty-two miles away at the other end of Lake Kivu. However, the road to Goma was barely passable, and the quickest way to make the trip was by commercial speedboat, called the *Fast Ferry*, that required a chilly, three-hour ride down the lake. I had never imagined I would be cold in the tropical DRC, but I shivered in a T-shirt all the way to Goma.

In Goma I met with two Dutch filmmakers, Ilse and Femke van Velzen (figure 7.3). They were identical twins who had produced *Breaking the Silence*, a documentary about rape in the DRC. The film aimed to overcome the societal taboo that prevented rape victims from talking about sexual violence. In the DRC women were frequently blamed for having been raped. Indeed, victims were regularly chased out of their homes by irate husbands and shamed into silence.

The film had been well-received in the West and had won awards at festivals, but the van Velzens very much wanted it also to have an impact in the DRC. There were virtually no cinemas or TV stations outside the major cities, so the van Velzens partnered with us to distribute the film through *mobile cinema* showings. These featured a large, inflated, plastic

FIGURE 7.3 The Van Velzen sisters, Dutch filmmakers.

screen that was usually set up in an open field. The film itself was shown by a video projector powered by a gasoline generator. The result looked something like a drive-in movie—except no one was in a car and the audience stood up to watch. In the entertainment-starved Congolese countryside, screenings attracted as many as 10,000 people, and our total audience was in the millions.

That night in a field outside Goma, I attended a mobile cinema showing of the van Velzen film. It was a powerful experience for me—and clearly cathartic for many in the crowd. I couldn't understand the soundtrack, which was in the local tribal language, but I could tell by the gasps and screams from the audience that the testimony on-screen from rape victims had a profound impact. After the film ended, our Congolese staff used microphones and loudspeakers to encourage local women to share their experiences, and many came forward with their own accounts of gender-based violence.

Because the van Velzens' film was so effective in reaching its audience, we decided to double-down and partner with the two sisters in adapting their next film, *Weapon of War: Confessions of Rape in Congo*, for use in our sensitization sessions for Congolese security forces. The sisters edited a new version, and it became an integral part of our program to retrain the Congolese Army and police.

When I arrived back in Goma, I had a very productive meeting with Ben Knapen, the Dutch Minister for International Cooperation, who was visiting some of his country's foreign aid projects. His ministry was already funding our programs in a major way, and I did not want to overload his systems by asking for more money. So I made what I thought was a yesable proposition that would be of great value to us and that would put Dutch officials into a leadership position among potential donors—and not cost them anything. My suggestion was for the Netherlands to convene other donors and encourage them to support us in expanding *Tomorrow Is a New Day* across the entire DRC. Sure enough, within a month I received an email from the Foreign Ministry in The Hague saying that Dutch diplomats had started to push the project with the British and Canadian aid agencies and that they planned to convene a meeting "to persuade" other donors to invest in our work. Although I cannot know what, if any, direct impact this Dutch assistance may have had, I am sure their support didn't hurt our standing with the rest of the funding community, and in the following months we received several large new grants.

The next day, Slachmuijlder and I flew on a UN plane to Kinshasa where we made a courtesy call on General Mulubi. I thanked him profusely for his seminal role in the *Tomorrow Is a New Day* program. Next, Slachmuijlder took me to meet with Search's TV production team. Although our media activities in the DRC began with radio, under her leadership we had expanded into television, which had a wide viewership in the DRC's twelve major cities. In Kinshasa alone, our programs reached about two million viewers. With TV as with radio, we functioned as a production studio, not a broadcaster.

With justifiable pride, our production team showed me samples of their output. One offering was a thirteen-episode dramatic series about the police. The hero was not a Commandant Janvier–type. Instead, he was a good cop who tried to do his job properly and who continually battled corruption and indifference. Every day he had to make difficult choices as he tried to act in an honest and upright way. Having made Commandant Janvier into a national villain, we wanted to create an even more powerful image of a policeman who acted in an exemplary way.

Our production team was also excited about a campaign underway to counter toxic masculinity. The goal was to popularize the idea that a Congolese could be a *real man* by respecting women and by saying "no" to exploitation and violence. Instead of condemning bad behavior, this series showed in positive ways that *real men* did not abuse women. Our short films were narrated by a well-known Congolese rapper, Celeo Scram, who drew the audience into the kind of situation that would typically lead to sexual violence (figure 7.4). However, no matter what the audience anticipated, in our films the storylines took a contrarian turn. In those days, well before #MeToo, we wanted to show how, even in a macho culture, masculinity did not require abusiveness. For instance, one film told the story of a young woman who was applying for a job in an office. She was afraid that the man who interviewed her had ulterior motives when he asked her to meet him in a hotel room that evening. Unfortunately, forcing women to have sex in return for employment was—and is—a common practice in the DRC. In our script, however, there was an unexpected ending. It turned out that the man had invited the woman to the hotel not for prurient reasons but to meet the office recruitment panel.

In addition, staff members described another series Search was producing. It was called *Tosalel'ango* (Let's Do It in Lingala), and it was the first reality series ever in the DRC. It showcased young people tackling actual

FIGURE 7.4 Celeo Scram: Are you a real man?

problems in their community. Shows demonstrated that it was possible to promote positive social change despite challenging conditions in the DRC. When we surveyed viewers to find out if this goal was being met, 98 percent answered that it was.

One episode of *Tosalel'ango* featured two female students named Jenny and Filston. Like most young women in the country, they had grown up in an environment where gender-based violence was endemic, and schoolgirls like them were frequent targets. Unscrupulous male teachers often pressured girls to trade sexual favors for passing marks. (The practice was informally known as *sexually transmitted grades*.) Jenny and Filston were convinced that something needed to be done about their predatory teachers, but they understood that directly approaching the authorities at their school or in their locality was probably not going to be effective. They reasoned that a way to make a yesable proposition to the powers that be was to appear on television and have the problem graphically displayed to a mass audience. They contacted the producers of *Tosalel'ango* and worked with our production team to make an episode about the abuses they had personally suffered and about the larger question of sexual violence in

Congolese schools. In this way, the girls were able to shame the authorities into action. After the episode was aired, the local police commander agreed to meet with them, and criminal charges were brought against four of their teachers. *Tosalel'ango* had called attention to a major societal problem, and Congolese teachers were put on notice that they could not continue to escape punishment when they committed crimes against their students.

After the session with the Search TV team, Slachmuijlder took me to meet the director of the television station in Kinshasa that was broadcasting *Tosalel'ango*. He praised the series heavily and said he wanted more such programming. We had clearly made him a proposition that was yesable both to him and to us. Here was the deal: We provided his station with popular, high-quality programming at no cost. In return, he agreed to broadcast the shows in prime time, and we at Search were able to reach a mass urban audience with programs that featured the ideas and values we wanted to communicate. Our donors were willing to say "yes" to our requests for funding because they were pleased with the effectiveness of what we were doing. It was definitely a *win-win-win*.

The TV station was my last stop on what was for me a magical mystery tour through the DRC. I witnessed the kind of work I had envisioned that Search would accomplish when I founded the organization. Particularly satisfying was the fact that—without direct input from me—Slachmuijlder had accomplished so much. I recognized that she had worked within the context of my vision and that she couldn't have done it without the organizational base Search provided. Like most successful social entrepreneurs and intrapreneurs, she had forged ahead when she saw openings, and to paraphrase Frank Sinatra, "she did it her way."

For the next year or two, I dined out on what I had witnessed in the DRC. I was proud to explain that Slachmuijlder had confirmed an idea I had strongly held to be true but had never before been able to verify: namely, that a societal approach to conflict prevention could work well in a geographically large country, and that even in a place as lawless as the DRC, skillfully crafted, yesable propositions could result in positive social change.

8

Practice Aikido

By nature, I am impatient. As a peacemaker and as a human being, I yearn for rapid outcomes to problems that are tearing apart the planet. In places like the Democratic Republic of Congo and Burundi, where my colleagues and I worked, there was widespread violence, and we were committed to doing everything we possibly could to end it. We understood, however, that even though we were the world's largest NGO in the peace-building field we were still a relatively small organization, and we lacked the power to reverse the course of events. As much as we opposed violence based on ethnic, religious, and gender differences, we realized that it was usually futile to take a confrontational stance. Literally and figuratively, screaming "STOP NOW!" only seemed to make matters worse.

If we had taken a directly adversarial position, we would have been acting like a boxer who tries to reverse the energy flow of an opponent—by knocking that person backward onto his or her rear end. We were convinced that such an approach was not an effective way to deal with conflicts—or with much of life, for that matter. Instead, we adopted a strategy rooted in aikido, a noncompetitive Japanese martial art (which literally translates as "the way of spirit harmony"). Aikido emphasizes accepting an attacker's incoming energy and awareness rather than countering with force and resistance. When we were involved in trying to end a violent conflict, we accepted as a given that we did not have the power to achieve our goal. We understood that we could only shift the conflict by ten or fifteen degrees, and we were always looking for innovative ways to cause that to happen. In essence, we were making a virtue out of necessity because we simply did not have the clout to act otherwise.

In aikido, the process of accepting the approach of an attacker and then diverting it is called the *blend.* It requires the practitioner to shift the attacking energy in a relatively small way—not to try, as a boxer would, to reverse it by 180 degrees. The result is to create a new *situation* in which the attacker and the individual being attacked both wind up in a position of safety. In my view, aikido offers an important conceptual metaphor for social entrepreneurs. They need to accept a situation as it is, blend with it, and transform it one step at a time.

I tried practicing aikido in the physical sense at a *dojo,* a place where martial arts were taught, but I did not like having my 6'3" frame thrown around on a mat—even though I knew I would be safe in the end. However, I realized that employing the core ideas that underlay aikido provided a key strategy—a *modus operandi*—for how social entrepreneurs could effectively operate and resolve conflicts. Principle #8 of social entrepreneurship is "practice aikido."

Lena Slachmuijlder used an aikido-type tactic in the DRC. Instead of directly confronting the Congolese Army and denouncing its atrocious record in abusing human rights, she accepted the army as it was and found small openings that eventually led to major change. Her nonadversarial methodology enabled her and her colleagues to carry out a program that retrained virtually the country's entire military. *Wrestling diplomacy* with Iran represented another example of aikido. Although it didn't directly take on the core problems between the United States and Iran, it opened up new possibilities for improving relations.

In Morocco, we also took an aikido-laden approach. We wanted to promote social and economic cohesion in the country. Instead of directly opposing the massive injustices and inequalities that existed there, we sought to shift the processes by which Moroccans resolved conflicts. Our goal was to create a culture in which disputes were resolved peacefully and in an equitable way.

Our program in Morocco began in the year 2000 at a time when the country was going through a major transition. Hassan II, the previous king, had died the year before. His son, Mohammed VI, was inclined, at least initially, to let a thousand flowers bloom as he tried to correct what the BBC called his father's "appalling human rights record." As Morocco was moving rapidly toward a more open political system, the country was experiencing the tensions that normally accompany processes of social change and democratization.

With all this going on, we received an unsolicited request to work in Morocco from Habib Belkouch, the director of the Ministry of Justice's Human Rights Center for Documentation, Information & Training. Belkouch had himself been imprisoned and tortured under the old regime. Now that he had been released and had become a government official, he believed that direct confrontation with the past was less likely to be successful than a more indirect approach. In other words, he had adopted a strategy that was consistent with aikido. He had learned about our work by participating in the Human Rights Working Group of our Middle East initiative. This group included Arabs, Israelis, and Iranians who cooperated to correct human rights abuses. He invited us to launch similarly inclusive programs in Morocco. His immediate target was the country's system for resolving labor disputes, which reflected long-standing adversarial patterns. After several preliminary visits, in 2001 we decided to open an office in Rabat, the capital city and begin a full program.

There had been a series of terrorist bombings in Morocco, but the country was mostly peaceful. The monarchy, whose lineage could be traced directly back to the Prophet Muhammad, was firmly in power. Several people asked us why Search, as a peace-building organization, chose to operate in a country where there was little violence. We answered that if nonviolent methods of dealing with differences were not applied to alleviate poverty and unrest, violence would eventually break out. We operated from the premise that the best time to prevent conflict was before it reached crisis proportions—in accordance with the old saying that "a stitch in time saves nine." In addition, if the methodology existed in a country to peacefully resolve contentious issues, we believed there was a good chance that it would be used. On the other hand, if methodology of this sort was not present, we surmised it almost certainly would not be brought to bear when conflicts arose.

Our presence was welcomed by Moroccan authorities, and they were more than willing to work with us. After all, Morocco was a country where absolute power rested with the monarchy, and our approach, which stressed *win-win* solutions and peaceful coexistence, was not threatening to the powers that be. We wanted to bring about profound change by gently shifting the way Moroccans dealt with their differences but without confrontation. Our approach represented aikido in action.

Disputes in Morocco traditionally had been dealt with by old and wise local leaders—mostly tribal chiefs and imams—who served as arbitrators and mediators between conflicting parties. They were called *judges*, and they were elected every three years, usually only by men who were over the age of forty. Many were paid by the government to go to their town's *souk* (marketplace) every week and resolve problems. Their rulings on issues such as quarrels over money, land ownership, and water rights were not legally binding, but the judges usually were able to find solutions. As Morocco had modernized, however, this ancient system for conflict resolution had mostly disappeared. We thought it was possible to reintroduce this methodology by combining it with contemporary techniques of mediation. At the same time, we needed to make sure that such a combination would not be too caught up in cultural biases. We tried to find the right mix between old and new, Moroccan and Western.

With funding from the U.S. State Department and the UK government, our first project was to support passage of a new labor law. The existing law was heavily weighted in favor of management, and it was usually backed up by government pressure against the workers. We carried out a series of consultations with key parties to determine the shape of a new law, and we provided training in more equitable forms of labor negotiations. We brought international negotiation experts to Morocco, and we organized study trips to Washington, D.C. and London of key players from government, unions, and management. Our activities were designed to build consensus around provisions of labor legislation that would be less adversarial than the existing law and would establish a fairer system of collective bargaining. In the end, our work directly contributed to passage of an updated labor law. This new law specifically included mediation as a means for resolving workplace disputes. As Oussama Safa, our country director in Morocco at the time, put it, "We were the catalysts in passing it."

In addition, we promoted mediation in the *bidonvilles*, the poverty-wracked shantytowns on the outskirts of Casablanca and other large cities. These places were breeding grounds for radicalism. One of our first projects was in Sidi Moumen, a slum area where there had been several suicide bombings that exploded not far from the cosmopolitan center of

Casablanca. Our core premise was that the attackers in Sidi Moumen were driven by problems caused by poverty, unemployment, and ideology, and we would provide tools for tackling these problems. We needed to overcome the hostility that separated the have-nots from the haves in communities like this. We saw such efforts as key to providing opportunity and lifting up those at risk, particularly young people. In partnership with the Moroccan government's Initiative for Human Development, we created community mediation centers in Sidi Moumen and in two other slum neighborhoods. We also provided training in mediation and coaching to 105 youth leaders.

"Mediation helps us resolve conflicts in a nonviolent manner," said twenty-two-year-old Zachariah who went through our training, "I want to show others that it can change their lives." Zachariah spoke in the face of skepticism from fellow community members who doubted that mediation would make any difference, but he and the other young mediators persisted. They carried out an awareness-raising campaign to show young people that there were alternatives to frustration and violence. The idea was to make Sidi Moumen into a more hopeful place. There was a profound need for change to enable people within the community to shape their destiny. Before the bombings "Sidi Moumen was ignored," said Hanan, another twenty-two-year-old. "I would like to show that within our community we have some very educated, intelligent, and motivated people."

When Susan Collin Marks and I made a site visit to one of the community centers Search had started, we talked at length with young mediators. They explained, step by step, how Searchers had taught them the finer points of mediation. Susan told them they were doing exactly what she did in her work, often at the highest levels of international affairs. Astonished and delighted, they beamed and poured out stories of their successes. One girl told us how she had been able to mediate between pupils and teachers—and even pupils and their parents. This was a big deal in Morocco's hierarchical society, where young people—particularly girls—did not normally become involved in a significant way with adults. As one of the youthful mediators said, "Our lives are completely different now. They are different in everything—in school, in associations, and in our families." In the words of a young woman, "Before it seemed that power and authority were the best mechanism for resolving disputes, and mediation was the domain for the authorities and tribal leaders. Now there is equality between people in mediation as a new way of conflict resolution."

In all, the young mediators were successful in using mediation to resolve more than one thousand cases with a success rate that at times reached nearly 90 percent. Of the mediated cases, 60 percent were school conflicts, 25 percent were neighborhood conflicts, and 15 percent were family conflicts. Our youthful colleagues established mediation cells at five high schools in Casablanca, and they founded their own organization, *Association Marocaine des Jeunes Médiateurs* (Moroccan Association of Youth Mediators). As yet another trainee put it, "Now I have learned to manage my own emotions. I no longer get overwhelmed with conflicts, and this helps me act in the right way in case of disagreement."

Our next major project in Morocco involved the courts. A judicial system had been established under the French colonial protectorate, and it had continued to exist after 1956 when the country became fully independent, But the courts were overwhelmed. According to the Ministry of Justice, three million new cases were filed annually. It usually took several years for a case to be decided, and the cost was beyond the reach of most of the population. The ministry estimated that about 60 percent of these cases could be resolved more quickly and economically through mediation, and making mediation widely available would significantly improve the judicial system. The arguments for increased use of mediation were not based on financial considerations alone but also on claims that it offered a more constructive way of resolving disputes. Success needed to be judged by the satisfaction of the parties.

In 2003, King Mohammed VI recognized that there were large problems in the Moroccan judicial system, and he called for upgrading and transforming it. In response to his royal edict, the Ministry of Justice signed an agreement with Search to provide training and advice for bringing mediation into the legal system (figure 8.1). Mediation was being used effectively in the United States and Europe to lighten court dockets and to find fair solutions to disputes. We were determined to institutionalize it in Morocco.

Our strategy for the judicial system included strategic planning, capacity-building, and a national consensus process aimed at bringing all relevant stakeholders on board. Accordingly, we worked with the Ministry of Justice to sponsor a series of training programs and forums for five hundred lawyers, magistrates, civil society leaders, parliamentarians, and private sector representatives. We also made use of TV and radio talk shows; we published a mediation guide; we used comic books to reach children and

FIGURE 8.1 John Marks signs the mediation agreement with Moroccan Minister of Justice Mohammed Bouzoubaa as the UK Ambassador Charles Gray looks on.

people who could not read; and we held simulations that were recorded on DVDs. Almost all the participants in our training programs, which were the first ever held in Morocco, were enthusiastic about what they learned. The only negative feedback came from a few attorneys who feared that introduction of mediation in Morocco would reduce their billings. As one lawyer put it, "If the mediation process is to marginalize lawyers, then I am against the reform. The reform should not have a negative impact on lawyers' revenues." We did not share that view. In the end, the lawyers mostly came on board, and the Moroccan bar association changed its bylaws to allow lawyers to serve as mediators.

In 2007, as a direct result of our joint efforts with the Ministry of Justice, the Moroccan Parliament passed a law that authorized mediation "as a voluntary, amicable, and confidential, out-of-court mechanism of dispute settlements." Needless to say, we were thrilled with this outcome. According to Mohammed Belmahi, a lawyer who had learned about mediation through our programs and who is today president of the Moroccan Mediation Authority, "It is thanks to Search for Common Ground that this concept has been re-invented in Morocco. . . . first by popularization of the concept and then by hundreds of trainings carried out in partnerships."

As was the case in the Democratic Republic of Congo, our Morocco program was implemented with little direct input from me in Washington, D.C. Our staff of Moroccans was calling the shots, and they were all under the age of thirty. Morocco was—and is—a country in which youth customarily had little voice; but these energetic young people believed passionately in what they were doing, and they had an extraordinary impact.

In 2008, in partnership with the national prison administration and the king's foundation for the reintegration of detainees, we began a new initiative to defuse extremism in Moroccan prisons. Even more than slums, prisons served as training grounds for violent behavior. Difficult living conditions, particularly overcrowding, exposed both inmates and guards to significant risks. In Morocco, as in most countries, prison staff had limited resources to manage the danger. Individual conflicts and tensions among detainees and guards frequently occurred. However, we had an alternative vision about what could happen in the country's prisons. We believed that prisons could be places of growth and rehabilitation. This vision was informed by South Africa's Robben Island where Nelson Mandela and much of the ANC's leadership had been incarcerated during the apartheid years. Despite the dreadful conditions there, prisoners had a profound learning experience. Many called the prison their "university."

In Moroccan prisons, our goal was to provide inmates with constructive approaches for dealing with conflict. We were not confronting potential terrorists through standard counterterrorism methods involving punitive or security measures. Rather, we were taking a long-range approach that focused on shifting the attitudes and behaviors of the prisoners. We wanted to increase their self-esteem and, in the process, lower their susceptibility to radical pressures. In addition to working with inmates, we included prison guards who were under a great deal of stress and whose attitudes and behaviors had a substantial impact on prison inmates.

Over the years, our program trained nearly two thousand inmates, fifty-five prison directors, and more than 150 staff members in forty-two prisons throughout Morocco. We had the support of the government and full access to prisoners and staff in more than half of the country's prisons. In 2012, we brought into the program two additional partners, the National Council for Human Rights and the *Rabita Mohammedia des Oulémas*.

The *Rabita* was a progressive network that included 1,300 imams and researchers who worked out of fifteen research centers across Morocco. Its mission was "to promote a tolerant and open Islam," and it worked from the premise that human rights were an integral part of the religion. Its head was—and is—Ahmed Abaddi, a charismatic, brilliant leader who was a close friend of mine and Susan's. In 2011, I approached Abaddi with the idea that the *Rabita* and Search could cooperate to carry out programs that combined modern conflict resolution techniques with traditional Islamic teaching. He agreed, and it was the beginning of a productive partnership. Before our two organizations began to cooperate, the *Rabita* was primarily a scholarly body. We played a key role in empowering the *Rabita* to also become an activist NGO involved in resolving critical problems and preventing violence. As Abaddi put it in an interview years later, "The dynamic was already there. Search brought the flame."

With the *Rabita*, our role was to find funding, furnish organizing skills, and help design training courses. The *Rabita* brought content and context in deconstructing extremism. Its approach fit well with Moroccan culture and sensibilities. Abaddi said, "For us, extremism is a disease." He was committed to bringing forth "an alternative discourse" among prisoners—and among the rest of the Moroccan population as well.

Together, the *Rabita* and Search developed a curriculum for a two-day training program for Moslem religious figures. It featured numerous examples of how the Prophet Mohammad himself used dispute resolution methodology to prevent violence between warring tribes. Abaddi concluded, "It was a great collaboration." We trained a total of 271 imams, scholars, and *mourchidates* (female teachers). They, in turn, passed on their teaching and training in deconstructing extremism to approximately 22,000 Moroccans.

In 2016, we at Search ended our work in Moroccan prisons. However, the *Rabita* not only continued the prison program but also collaborated with other partners to extend the training to all of the country's seventy-eight jails. In addition, the *Rabita* applied the methodology it had developed with us to expand its programs to schools, universities, and the media. It also carried out nationwide projects to reduce violence against women and, generally, to enhance the feminine role in Moroccan society. Although Search is no longer directly involved, our work with the *Rabita* continues to resonate to this day.

In conclusion, we at Search can take satisfaction in having brought modern forms of conflict resolution to Morocco. According to Mohammed Belmahi, head of the Moroccan Mediation Authority, as of 2022 more than one thousand professionals were making a living as mediators and dispute resolvers in the country. When we began, there had been none. For many years, we were the sole organization that provided training in mediation and conflict resolution. Today mediation has become firmly entrenched and institutionalized in the legal, social, and economic fabric of the country. Mediators are called upon regularly to help settle conflict in the judicial, business, and financial sectors. Indeed, mediation has become so mainstream that the Moroccan Olympic Committee has written mediation into its charter for dealing with disputes involving athletes; and Royal Air Maroc, the national airline, uses it to settle complaints from passengers. Even divorce mediation has come to Morocco.

Our aim from the beginning was to bring a culture of mediation to Morocco. It would seem that we were successful.

9

Develop Effective Metaphors

Principle #9 of social entrepreneurship is "develop effective metaphors." The goal is to transmit key messages in a convincing way. Extended metaphors, usually in the form of compelling stories, can play a key role in breaking up—and replacing—deeply held beliefs. To accept new ideas, most people need to be confident that there is a feasible alternative. Graphic storytelling can accomplish this and contribute to substantial belief changes. Metaphors—short or lengthy—provide a picture of what might lie ahead and why it is desirable.

Social entrepreneurs need to be able to tell their stories in visual, written, and spoken terms. They should be skilled practitioners of what advertising executives call *content marketing*. Above all they must be able to plausibly and clearly answer this question: "What would the new reality look like?"

The medium—or combination of media—that works best to communicate new possibilities would seem to depend on the mindset of those in the target audience. Some people are most affected by the written or spoken word. Others are more moved by what they see or hear.

Music can penetrate consciousness in a profound way, and we Searchers produced peace songs in many of the places where we worked. The music video we made in Angola became the theme song for that country's

FIGURE 9.1 Salman Ahmad and Melissa Etheridge sing for peace on Search music video. *Source*: Photo by Patty Hoaglund.

constitutional reform process. In Egypt, national television regularly played our song calling for understanding between Moslems and Christians whenever there was a violent incident. American icon Melissa Etheridge and Pakistani rock star Salman Ahmad made a music video for us that was shown around the world (figure 9.1).

I was always on the lookout for convincing metaphors—particularly those that operated on both the intellectual and the emotional level. In the early days of Search, I regularly stood up in living rooms and compared the U.S.-Soviet relationship to two boys standing knee-deep in a room full of gasoline—each holding a different number of matches. I said that Search's aim was not to change the mix of matches but to find ways to drain the gasoline from the room. This metaphor illustrated the need for a fundamental shift in the framework within which the United States and the USSR confronted each other. For many listeners, it provided an understanding of how the Cold War could possibly be transformed. I wanted to communicate that Search could play a part in making this happen, and I hoped that people in my audience would support our work.

Whenever possible in these sessions, I used short videos to supplement the message I wanted to deliver. At the same time, I recognized that person-to-person encounters of this sort only reach small groups of people. Similarly, the workshops and trainings Search sponsored typically involved no more than twenty-five individuals at a time. Certainly, there could be what Robert Kennedy called a "ripple" effect, but even that was unlikely to reach a mass audience.

I had a lofty vision of transformation, but to have an impact at the global level I clearly needed be able to move beyond workshops, trainings, and books, which did not reach the millions of people I wanted to influence. I concluded that, at least for me, the best way to do this was to make extensive use of mass media—a realization that predated 1982, the year I founded Search. My defining experience had come three years earlier while I was writing my second book, *The Search for the "Manchurian Candidate."* At that time, the *Close-Up* division of ABC News asked if I would collaborate in producing a TV documentary about the CIA's mind control programs, which were the subject of my book. ABC agreed that the documentary would be drawn mainly from material in my manuscript, and the program would be broadcast at the time of the book's publication. I very much liked the idea, if for no other reason than I thought a televised version of the book would greatly expand readership. In addition, I had no previous experience in television, and I wanted to learn how to be a TV producer.

I made an agreement with ABC to be a consultant for the documentary and gave ABC access to my manuscript prior to publication. The deal stipulated that whenever ABC made use of information taken from the book I would either be interviewed on camera or the narrator would credit the book. In addition, ABC agreed that I could accompany camera crews on shoots and be present in the edit suite, so I could gain knowledge in TV production. However, I did not have what television professionals call *final cut.* I was only an observer with a steep learning curve.

When the documentary aired, it was seen by about eight million viewers. Although ABC was disappointed with that number, I noted that the audience was about 7,970,000 more people than had read the book. I recognized that TV could hold a magnifying glass over my work and make it available to a large number of people. That lesson remained with me after I founded Search, and it informed my belief that media could play a key part in defusing conflict. Instead of being part of the problem—which media programming so often had been—I believed media could be part of the solution.

However, my strategy did not include writing another book and having it made into a TV program. Nor did I think I would be particularly successful in using public relations techniques to bring attention to my work. I found my answer in an insight famously expressed by A. J. Liebling, the New Yorker's longtime press critic. He said, "Freedom of the press is guaranteed only to those who own one." Taking this insight to heart, I decided that, in addition to our other activities, we Searchers would start our own TV production department and produce programming that promoted peaceful conflict resolution.

In 1986, four years after I founded Search, I created a division inside the organization called Common Ground Productions (CGP). At the beginning, CGP had no reality, although I had a grand vision of making broadcast-quality media programming that delivered high-impact, behavior-changing messages. I imagined that CGP would provide viewers with what was, in essence, electronic therapy. I wanted to take advantage of the fact that every culture has a storytelling tradition. I foresaw CGP making programs that combined local values with modern media production techniques. The ultimate goal would be to reach a mass audience with programming that would promote positive social change.

My first step in bringing this vision to life was to have business cards printed that said I was the president of Common Ground Productions. I fully understood that printing shops that make business cards do not ask for proof or credentials. All they required was to be paid for the cost of the cards. By making a declaration that something exists, as I did when I ordered the cards, my vision took concrete form. These business cards began the progression that enabled CGP to move from pipe dream to international producer.

Only three years after the first cards came back from the printer, CGP produced a ten-part series that aired on more than one hundred U.S. public TV stations. The series was called—of all things—*Search for Common Ground*. William Ury, coauthor of *Getting to Yes*, helped us develop a format that worked in TV terms and was consistent with our name and values. The series featured facilitated discussions between public figures on opposing sides of contentious issues. Scott Simon of National Public Radio (NPR) was the host, and I was the on-air moderator.

The series did not overlook the disagreements, but the emphasis was on finding common ground. Our approach was different from the traditional journalistic practice of stressing conflict—often for its entertainment value. The guiding principle in many newsrooms was (and is) *if it bleeds, it leads.* In fact, most journalists seem to work from the premise that conflict is interesting, agreement is boring, and adversarial interaction draws the largest audience. As a result, media outlets tend to reward outrageous behavior with airtime and column inches, and they often ignore actions aimed at building consensus and solving problems.

Shows full of conflict may create lively conversations and raise ratings. However, a strong case can be made that programming of this sort increases polarization and has a negative impact on the country and the world. Societies almost certainly function better when differences are resolved and conflict is not exacerbated. Indeed, if solutions are going to be found to the ever-growing list of problems that face humanity, common sense would seem to call for reducing adversarial behavior.

Having once made my living as an investigative reporter who specialized in pointing out flaws in the system, I was now producing and moderating a TV series in which guests were asked to look beyond their differences and discover actual agreements.

The series had programs on issues such as abortion, euthanasia, and U.S.-Soviet relations. One particularly lively episode was called "What's the Common Ground on Gun Control." The guests were Wayne LaPierre, then the chief lobbyist of the National Rifle Association (NRA) and subsequently its director, and Pete Shields, who headed Handgun Control and whose son had been killed by gun violence (figure 9.2). These two men had appeared together many times. Normally people like them were used by media to engage in battles of opposing sound bites. They were pros, and an important part of their job was to present their organization's views to the public. To be featured in the media, as they clearly wanted to be, they needed to be articulate and dynamic. In contrast, as a producer for the popular news series *Nightline* once confided to me, if potential guests were suspected of wanting to find common ground, they would not be invited to appear on the program.

In the opening segment of our show, Scott Simon narrated an introduction that framed the core question thusly: "Does gun control reduce crime, or does gun control only keep guns out of the hands of law-abiding citizens?" Then he turned over to me what seemed like the difficult task

FIGURE 9.2 On U.S. public TV, John Marks finds common ground between Pete Shields (left) of Handgun Control and Wayne LaPierre of the NRA.

of finding common ground. To begin, I asked LaPierre to briefly state his basic position. At this point, the show deviated from the norm. Instead of having Shields do the same, I asked him, as he had been forewarned I would, to restate LaPierre's position—to LaPierre's satisfaction. Next, the process was reversed, with Shields stating his basic position and LaPierre repeating it to Shields's satisfaction. This repetition of the other's position was important because it required both guests to listen carefully rather than to be thinking ahead to what they were going to say next. When people do not listen, there is little chance for them to find common ground.

Despite being willing to appear together, LaPierre and Shields showed little respect for each other, and they profoundly disagreed about how to deal with guns. Nevertheless, it was not our intention to stage a debate in the usual sense. We were looking for something else, and we kept score on an electronic scoreboard (figure 9.3). Each time our guests found a point of agreement, it was noted on the scoreboard. When they agreed that they disagreed, that was also recorded on the scoreboard.

LaPierre's solution to the problem of gun violence was to build more prisons and strengthen the punitive measures to be taken against criminals. Shields, for his part, supported restrictions on what kind of guns could be

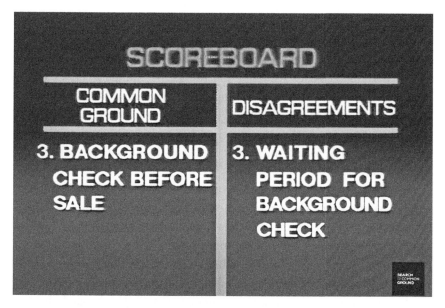

FIGURE 9.3 Keeping score on an electronic scoreboard, Search style.

sold and who could own them. But their core disagreement was only the starting point, and the program then moved on to the next question, which was almost never asked: In view of your massive disagreements, are there any areas on which you might agree?

There were some easy agreements. Both men concurred that the other side was extreme and distorted their position. However, both said that they did not distort the views of the other side. In addition, they agreed that automatic weapons, plastic pistols, and *cop-killer* ammunition should be banned; that criminals should not have access to weapons; that there should be instantaneous background checks before sales; that there should be tough penalties for criminal use of guns; and that carriers of concealed weapons could be licensed and made to undergo training in gun safety. Most important, they said they could jointly support a package that included instantaneous background checks, more jails, and a tougher criminal justice system. As Scott Simon put it at the end of the program:

> If the two sides in the gun control controversy can join together to design and support such a program, there may be a better climate to deal with what is the deeper question: How to prevent so many Americans from shooting each other.

By simply getting the *Search for Common Ground* series on the air, CGP took a major leap forward. With this series under our collective belts, we were well on the way to becoming a credible TV production company. But we had higher goals. Among other things, we wanted to create a new model for TV talk shows, and we hoped our discussion format would be replicated across the United States. Unfortunately, despite our best efforts, that never happened. However, we had better luck internationally, and we used the same format in producing series in Russia, Sri Lanka, and Macedonia.

In 1993 I received an invitation from Hannes Siebert, head of South Africa's Media Peace Center, to come to Cape Town to produce a *Search for Common Ground* TV series. While apartheid had gripped South Africa, I had avoided working there. I had not thought there could be any common ground that included the apartheid regime, and I had not wanted to be co-opted. Now Nelson Mandela had been released from prison, and the country was transitioning to democracy. Given the changed circumstances, I eagerly accepted Siebert's invitation and flew off to South Africa for a trip that would change my life very much for the better.

Within days of arriving in Cape Town, not only did I meet my future wife, then Susan Collin, but Siebert and I worked out the details for coproducing a ten-part series to be called *South Africa Searches for Common Ground* (figure 9.4). Siebert wanted the series to be broadcast by NNTV, part of the SABC national network, and he felt that I, as an American who had produced a similar series, should pitch the series to the SABC leadership. So Siebert arranged a lunch for me in Johannesburg with the network's chief programming executive. This man proved to be an easy sell, and he agreed to air the series even before our food was served.

With the deal in hand and the reason for the lunch concluded, it would have been massively impolite for me to leave before the end of the meal. I felt a need to make conversation with the SABC man, a taciturn Afrikaner, but I quickly ran out of small talk. Somewhat desperate for subjects to discuss, I took a chance and decided to push him beyond what I thought might be his comfort zone. I asked if he was familiar with *Eyes on the Prize*, the award-winning PBS series on the history of the American civil rights movement. To my surprise he replied that SABC had previously tried to buy the series, but its producers had refused to sell it to a TV network that was part of the apartheid regime. I replied that with the African National Congress (ANC) no longer banned and apartheid on its

FIGURE 9.4 *South Africa Searches for Common Ground*—the TV series.

way out, circumstances probably had changed. He threw the ball back to me and said, if I could arrange it, SABC would certainly be interested in airing the series.

Selling another producer's TV series did not seem to be part of my job description, but I believed *Eyes on the Prize* could make a real difference in South Africa. Therefore, when I returned to the United States, I made a cold call to Henry Hampton, the series' legendary executive producer. Now that apartheid was ending, I asked if he would be willing to sell the series to SABC. Under these new circumstances, he said he would be glad to, so I put him in touch directly with SABC. Soon, all fourteen episodes of *Eyes on the Prize* were aired in South Africa, and I was thrilled to have made the connection. Hampton even insisted that Search be paid the standard 10 percent agent's fee for setting up the sale. This was an unanticipated windfall, and we used the money to produce more common ground programming. Once again, being engaged led to unexpected opportunities.

Another unforeseen development was the emergence of radio as a key part of our media toolbox. When I started CGP, I mistakenly thought we would only be a TV producer. But I came to see that in many less-developed countries, particularly those in conflict, radio was the best way to reach the masses. In much of Africa, TV was, in fact, a minor or nonexistent player. CGP's first foray into radio had been with Studio *Ijambo* in Burundi in 1995 (see chapter 6). A year later, I received an unsolicited phone call from the Netherlands. Jan Pronk, then the Dutch Minister of Development Cooperation, knew all about Studio *Ijambo*, and he wanted us to set up a similar facility in Liberia, which was then coming out of a bloody civil war.

Minister Pronk's request posed a dilemma for us at Search. As an organization, one of our basic rules was that we would not let the availability of money drive our programming. Now the Dutch government was offering to provide funds that would allow us to start operations in a new country. My colleagues and I discussed at length whether to accept the money. We concluded that a radio studio in Liberia along the lines that Pronk was proposing was conceptually identical to Studio *Ijambo* in Burundi, and that the need for such a studio was at least as great in war-torn Liberia as it had been in Burundi. As a result, we decided it would be foolish to turn down a grant that was consistent with our vision just because a funder had proposed it. So we said thank-you very much, and we accepted the Dutch money to set up *Talking Drum* Studio—talking drums having traditionally been a prime means of communication in Liberia and throughout West Africa.

Once our Liberian studio was operational, its programs attracted an audience of 90 percent of the people of Monrovia, the capital city where half of the population lived. Subsequently we used our base in Liberia to start full country programs in Sierra Leone, Côte d'Ivoire, and Guinea. In all those places, we set up radio studios and carried out a wide range of other peace-building activities.

As our radio production grew, we also increased our television output in countries where TV played a major role. Our first TV programs had been facilitated talk shows; although they were informative, we realized that they were hardly popular entertainment. We very much wanted to reach an even larger audience, and we saw would have to produce more engaging programming to do that—including dramatic series, reality shows, and documentaries.

These other formats were more expensive than talk shows, but we had built up sufficient credibility as a TV producer that we were increasingly able to attract funding. For example, our series in South Africa, which had featured studio-based discussions, led directly in 1997 to USAID support for our most ambitious production yet, a thirteen-episode documentary series we coproduced with Ubuntu Films. It was filmed in thirteen different countries and highlighted traditional and modern ways of resolving conflict across the African continent. One episode from Mozambique told the story of a former child soldier who wanted to return to his home village but was not welcome because he had been a killer. He was allowed back finally after the local shaman put him through a purification ritual that involved breaking off the head of a chicken. Another program filmed in South Africa featured a more up-to-date form of conflict resolution. It showcased how providing video cameras to gang leaders was able to defuse ethnic violence.

We made English, French, and Portuguese versions of these series, which were aired all over Africa. The *Cape Argus* newspaper wrote, "The series seeks to shed light on what is working and what is not, to challenge old stereotypes and assumptions, and to provide new ways of thinking about conflicts and new tools for dealing with them."

When Susan and I moved to Jerusalem in 2002, we formed an enduring partnership with Palestine's Ma'an Media Network and its general director, Ra'ed Othman, a social entrepreneur par excellence. He started as a tiny broadcaster who pirated much of his early programming, and he grew to become Palestine's largest media producer. Our first encounter with him came during the second intifada when he agreed to broadcast *A Force More Powerful*, an American documentary series on nonviolence. At that point, he invited Susan and me to come to Ramallah for the initial meeting of the Palestinian mom-and-pop television stations he was in the process of bringing into the Ma'an TV network. As we met with Othman and the station managers, we got a worried call from a Canadian diplomat who had given us a ride into Ramallah in an armored SUV. He said Israeli tanks were rolling into the city, and it wasn't safe for us to remain. He sent the SUV to collect us immediately.

We were not deterred by this armed interruption, nor was Othman. From that beginning, we wound up working with Ma'an to coproduce scores of dramatic programs, talk shows, and a news magazine along the lines of *60 Minutes*. In addition, we aided Ma'an in producing a daily news series that continues to this day. We even coproduced our first-ever reality series titled *The President*. It was a thirty-episode series that used an elimination format like *American Idol*'s to select a young person to be Palestine's next president (figure 9.5). More than 1,200 potential candidates signed up to be contestants. The winner was selected by viewers who *voted* with

FIGURE 9.5 A Palestinian presidential *candidate* faces the judges on the reality series titled *The President*.

SMS text messages for the person who had the qualities they hoped to see in their president. The ratings were extraordinary: one million Palestinian households—roughly half the population—watched the series.

In addition to reality programming, we also made a major expansion into drama, and that attracted large audiences. Our core premise was that entertaining, nondidactic, dramatic programming could have a profound impact on how people thought about themselves, their neighbors, and their society. I was inspired by shows such as *All in the Family*, whose lead character was Archie Bunker. I believed this series and others produced by Norman Lear had played a major role in shifting mass views on bigotry and racism in the United States. Repetition seemed to me to be a key reason these multi-episodic series could have such a pronounced impact. With a new episode every week, viewers welcomed characters into their living rooms with whom they could identify and empathize.

Our first TV dramatic series, *Nashe Maalo*, aired in Macedonia in 1998, and we produced it in partnership with the producers of *Sesame Street* (see chapter 5). Three years later we again collaborated with *Sesame*, this time in Cyprus where we made an eight-part series called *Gimme 6*. This series featured a Greek Cypriot boy who went to England to attend a summer soccer camp and met a Turkish Cypriot girl who was going to music school. The two of them became close friends, and they in turn got involved with a larger, multicultural group of kids. The series was broadcast on both the Greek and Turkish sides of Cyprus, as well as in mainland Greece and Turkey.

Next came a forty-nine-episode dramatic series in Nigeria called *The Station*. Making a TV series there presented unexpected difficulties. We converted a dilapidated Lagos warehouse into a production studio, and that required the removal of a nest of cobras from behind what became the soundstage. Less dangerous but still problematic was the tin roof. When it rained hard, the clattering on the metal made it impossible to shoot until the weather cleared—which wasn't so often during the rainy season.

This Nigerian series told the story of a fictional TV news station in Lagos—imagine a Nigerian CNN. The boss was a Muslim woman who wore a modern hijab. Her multiethnic, multireligious staff reported on the most urgent problems the country faced—through a prism of tolerance. Their struggle to cooperate was symbolic of the need for Nigerians from all groups to come together. Beyond social and political issues, the series also dealt with the drama of daily life, the stuff of soap opera. Nestlé sponsored the series, and it was featured at the Clinton Global Initiative. Former President Bill Clinton called the series "exciting." He added, "I might like to see one of these [series] in America."

Our TV news format was well received in Nigeria, and we thought it could be popular elsewhere. We got our chance when Mohamed Gohar, the owner of a television production company in Cairo, heard about the series and offered to coproduce an Egyptian version. That seemed like a good idea, particularly because Gohar's company, Video Cairo Sat, had the resources and experience to make such a series. We sent English-language scripts from Lagos to Cairo, and Egyptian screenwriters linguistically and culturally translated them. *The Station*'s reporters became Muslims and Coptic Christians, instead of Yorubas and Hausas. The result was a thirty-episode, Arabic-language series that aired on Egyptian national television and on satellite TV across the entire Middle East.

In 2006, we developed a new format that enabled us to become a global producer. It came about when one of our interns came to see me with a keen insight. At that time, the World Cup in soccer was only months away from starting in Germany. The intern pointed out that soccer—or football, as most of the world calls it—almost always trumps politics, and that the World Cup would be watched by billions of viewers. He asked, "What are we doing to take advantage of it?" I replied, "Nothing." Then, I added, "But we should do something." And during the next few minutes, a new format was born.

I had launched wrestling diplomacy with Iran eight years earlier, and I had come to see that sport could be a powerful tool for peace building. In that year of the World Cup, I reasoned why not combine soccer, the world's most popular sport, with dramatic television programming, one of the world's most popular entertainment forms. This insight led to a TV series called *The Team* (figure 9.6). In each country where we produced

FIGURE 9.6 *The Team*, a TV series in eighteen countries featuring a fictional soccer team reflecting diversity.

this series, the action centered on a fictional soccer team that reflected the diversity of that country. Of course, as with most Search programs, there were exceptions. In Pakistan and Sri Lanka, where soccer was not king, our series focused on a cricket team.

We had a large vision for the series. But without funding in hand, we had no choice but to start small. That meant beginning with radio in a country where we were already working. In 2006 in Côte d'Ivoire, we produced *The Team* as a twenty-six-part radio drama. It focused on two soccer players who came from different regions and ethnic groups. Like many African stars, they competed professionally in Europe and played together on the Ivoirian national team. The BBC described the series as "entertaining and humorous, whilst communicating a message of reconciliation."

After *The Team* aired in Côte d'Ivoire, we felt that the format was ready for primetime TV, but we still didn't have the needed funds. We thought that our best bet for finding the money would be to make a proposal to the UK's Department for International Development (DFID). After all, the Brits seemed to have a fondness for the idea that multi-episodic soap opera could be used to promote social change. In 1951, the BBC invented the genre when it produced *The Archers*, a daily radio serial that instructed farmers on how to increase their agricultural output. More than seventy years later, *The Archers* is still airing six days a week, and it has expanded to deal with many other issues.

In view of this history, we asked DFID for $6.1 million to produce *The Team* in ten African, Middle Eastern, and Asian countries—without specifying which countries. The funding gods were clearly aligned with us because DFID said "yes." For the first time ever, we had a seven-figure pot of money and flexibility on where we could spend it.

Moreover, with this grant in hand, I was not content to stop fundraising for the series. Like most people, I was convinced that those who have money are more likely to get more money. Thus I made a declaration to my fellow Searchers: we would use the DFID grant as leverage to double the funds available for production of *The Team*, and we would produce the series in more countries than we had originally promised. Happily my declaration turned out to be an underestimation. We wound up more than tripling the DFID grant, thanks to the generosity of eleven additional funders. Altogether we produced 356 episodes of *The Team* in eighteen countries.

In each place where we made the series, we found a local NGO or production house with sufficient technical skills to be our coproducer. In addition, we always enrolled a national TV network in the target country to serve as broadcaster. This was not too difficult because in most developing countries little drama was actually being produced. Station managers primarily bought foreign programming—mostly schlocky U.S. or European fare—for a price considerably lower than what it would cost to produce original programming in that country. We devised a business model that almost always resulted in a yesable proposition that was accepted by prospective broadcasters. We offered them a high-quality, locally produced dramatic series at no cost. In a few places, we even paid for airtime. In return, the broadcaster agreed to publicize the series and show it in prime time.

Each production of *The Team* needed to reflect the culture of the country in which it was being made. This could not be accomplished with scripts written in faraway places, so we employed local writers. At the same time, we wanted to make sure the plots reflected our common ground perspective. We understood that compelling drama called for conflict between characters, but our shows did not allow violence to prevail. In the end, we wanted the good guys to win.

To make sure programs met our standards, we usually sent in Deborah Jones, who was then executive producer of Common Ground Productions. Jones was masterful in bringing out the best in local scriptwriters, and she guided them through a two-week workshop during which general storylines were developed. Afterward, she read and edited draft scripts until final versions were ready. In each country where she worked, she combined TV production skills with a deep knowledge of our common-ground approach. Before coming to Search, she had worked in Hollywood where she had created a TV series called *Amazing Grace* starring Patty Duke. In addition, she had written several television films.

Despite Jones's successes in *La La Land*, she had come to feel that there was more to life than making made-for-TV movies, and she had enrolled in a master's program at Tufts University's Fletcher School to learn about conflict resolution. She was first recommended to us for a job as a summer intern. I initially met her on a trip to Boston, and she was the only prospective intern I ever encountered who arrived at her job interview in a Mercedes.

The first place we produced a televised version of *The Team* was in Kenya where we had an excellent local partner, Media Focus on Africa. Our broadcaster was Citizen-TV, the country's most watched television network. The series lasted for three seasons and consisted of thirty-nine

FIGURE 9.7 *The Team* cast in Kenya.

half-hour shows that consistently ranked in the top-ten of Kenyan TV programs. We also made radio versions of the series that were broadcast in tribal languages.

Like most countries in Africa, Kenya had a gender problem. Jones and the local writers came up with a plot premise in which a Kenyan team was invited to a seven-a-side soccer tournament that featured young women and men playing together as equals (figure 9.7). To top it off, the Kenyans had a woman coach, and the males on the team had to overcome their resistance to playing for her. Beyond gender issues, the series focused on the conflicts between the country's many ethnic groups, and team members all came from different tribes. The core metaphor of the series—in Kenya and everywhere—was that players who did not cooperate and overcome their ethnic and religious differences would not score goals, and they would lose. As former UN secretary-general Kofi Annan described *The Team* during the period when he served as a mediator to prevent violence in Kenya, "This timely, topical project is a very positive step forward in helping Kenyans to overcome obstacles such as ethnicity, which stand in the way of progress for the country."

FIGURE 9.8 *The Team* cast in Indonesia.

Everywhere we produced *The Team*, we homed in on local problems (figures 9.8 and 9.9). In the Democratic Republic of Congo, players were 100 percent women, and the series was part of our nationwide campaign to prevent sexual violence. In Côte d'Ivoire, the series explored divisions between Muslims and Christians. In Morocco, the gulf was between rich

FIGURE 9.9 *The Team* cast in Sri Lanka.

and poor. In Indonesia, the action was set inside a prison where convicts from two ethnic groups were fighting each other until a new warden—a woman—started a soccer team.

In 2013, I had an appointment at the USAID office in Cairo where I planned to pitch a Middle Eastern regional version of *The Team*. My interlocutor, a veteran USAID man, quickly told me he wasn't interested in a soccer-based series. He did ask, however, if I had anything in my bag of tricks that involved the empowerment of women. On the spot, I invented a new format. I told him that we could make a dramatic series called *Madam President*. I said that the series would be set in a fictional Arab country and would resemble the American TV show *The West Wing*—except that the president would be a woman. Unlike most of the male rulers in the region, she would be a problem-solver. She would eschew violence and would not base her policies on saving face or seeking revenge. The USAID man clearly had an urgent bureaucratic need for women's programming. Unknowingly I had ventured into his office at a crucial moment—presumably when he had money left in his budget that needed to be spent before the end of the fiscal year. He asked me to move quickly and to send him a concept note and a budget for the series I had just described. I did so, and USAID came through with a substantial grant.

Jones and I decided to base production of *Madam President* in Jordan, and the result was fifteen hours of dramatic programming that was broadcast across the entire Middle East by satellite TV. Subsequently we used a similar format in Nepal to produce a series called *Madame Prime Minister*.

Despite producing all of these TV series, Common Ground Productions had never made a feature film. That opportunity came in Jerusalem in 2013 when the European Union provided us with funding for an Israeli-Palestinian coproduction called *Under the Same Sun*. This was a fictional docudrama set in the near future. It told the story of two business partners: a Palestinian and an Israeli who formed a joint solar energy company. Because of objections in in each society to normalizing relations with the other side, they both faced profound hostility. They came to recognize that their business would have little chance of success if the conflict continued. Their solution was to mount a Facebook campaign that created a groundswell of support for a negotiated settlement. They had set out to make money, and they wound up making peace. The film—obviously a fable—aired on both Israel's Channel 2 and the Palestinian Ma'an Network, and it was shown repeatedly on American TV by Participant Media's Pivot Network.

By the time I stepped down as president of Search in 2014, media projects consumed about half of our budget. We pioneered the use of television and radio programming to promote social change, and our extensive use of media distinguished our work from other organizations in the peace-building field. As the *Christian Science Monitor* put it, "Search for Common Ground knows first-hand the subtle, healing power of storytelling."

10

Display *Chutzpah*

Social entrepreneurship is definitely not a good career choice for those who are timid. Launching new initiatives and overcoming seemingly insoluble problems often requires *chutzpah* (a Yiddish word meaning extreme self-confidence—or nerve or gall). When bold solutions are called for, social entrepreneurs need to exhibit sufficient chutzpah to take risks that facilitate pushing into unknown territory. Principle #10 of social entrepreneurship is "display chutzpah."

Nevertheless, chutzpah should not be seen as a boundless quality that social entrepreneurs regularly unleash. It should be a calculated response—and not one that is triggered by anger. It needs to be tempered with discretion and wisdom. In my view, both *good* and *bad* chutzpah exist. The most familiar example of bad chutzpah was described by author Leo Rosten: "Chutzpah is that quality enshrined in a man who, having killed his mother and father, throws himself on the mercy of the court as an orphan." In contrast, good chutzpah is what Abraham, the Biblical prophet, demonstrated when he had the effrontery to oppose God's plan to destroy Sodom and Gomorrah. By standing up to God, Abraham had the nerve to take a grave risk to save lives—even if the people spared were evil and corrupt.

Social entrepreneurs should avoid displaying bad chutzpah. No matter how worthy the cause, the ends do not justify the means. Needless to say, it is almost never OK to be rude or obnoxious in the name of making the world a better place. However, sometimes social entrepreneurs should dial up their inner chutzpah and act in a politely pushy manner. For example, I have found that bureaucrats, particularly those in government offices, tend to be overloaded with paperwork and meetings. When a social entrepreneur has submitted a proposal and has not received a response, it can be helpful, after a decent interval, to be insistent in seeking an answer. This tactic can sometimes move the proposal from the bottom of an inbox to the top. At other times, if the person being targeted feels unduly pressured, there can be an adverse reaction. In such a situation, I have found the best way to proceed is to be understanding and mildly apologetic. Rather than directly confronting a slow-moving official, I might communicate something like this: "Please excuse my pushiness. I know that you are very busy, but I would much appreciate it if you could let me know when you will be able to provide me with an answer."

In substantive matters, social entrepreneurs should be prepared to be daring and to take risks. The trick is to find the right balance between risk-taking and throwing caution to the wind. But even when social entrepreneurs take preventive measures that reduce the chances of failure, they should understand that a high percentage of their prospective undertakings are not going to be successful. I estimate that no more than one-third of the initiatives I proposed over the years were ever realized. A baseball player who hits .333 is a superstar, but this batting average also involves a large number of strikeouts. Social entrepreneurs, like superstars, must not allow themselves to be crippled by missed swings, which are very much part of the game. They need to be able to deal with failure, if for no other reason than because they have no other choice.

Founding Search for Common Ground was, on my part, an act of chutzpah. Like most social entrepreneurs in the start-up phase, I was putting my future on the line. I didn't have a Plan B. Search reflected my vision, but there was almost no evidence that the work I contemplated was feasible or even a good idea. In those pre-Google days, I consulted by phone and in person with knowledgeable people about what I wanted to do and what might be possible. I was able to borrow ideas from other groups, such as the Esalen Institute's Soviet-American initiative and Harvard's Project on Negotiation, but as far as I knew, no organization like Search had ever existed. In the end, I simply had to take a chance and dive in. Doing so turned out to be the best professional decision I ever made. I discovered my life's work.

The going was not easy in the early years before Search had much of a track record. We were carrying out only a few projects, and if one had failed, there would have been little else on which to fall back. I shudder to remember how I would sit in a workshop and worry that things were not going well. I feared that the meeting would crash and take the organization with it. However, I usually was able to shake this feeling by invoking a reassuring mantra: *trust the process.*

In those first days, Search was in a precarious position partly because of the difficulty my colleagues and I had in raising enough money to keep our doors open. We needed to pay for both operations and salaries. We realized that there was a fundamental contradiction in our early fund-raising strategy. All our funding came from the United States, but our approach seemed more compatible with the values of countries in northern Europe. We recognized that we needed to find ways to reach possible donors in the UK, the Netherlands, Belgium, and Scandinavia. Therefore, in 1994, shortly after I married Susan, she and I decided to travel together to Europe in search of funds. To paraphrase Willie Sutton, "Europe seemed to be the place where the money was."

Our strategy combined chutzpah with romance. As newlyweds, the idea of a trip together to Europe was exciting. But for purposes of fund-raising, we were heading into unexplored terrain, and we chose to proceed in a way that broke new ground. In keeping with the idea that 80 percent of success is showing up, we understood that we needed to meet in person with potential funders. We did our homework before we left Washington, D.C., and we put together a full schedule of appointments with the help of referrals from European friends and colleagues.

Because Search was a cash-starved organization, keeping costs down was a high priority. At the same time, for both Susan and me, taking long train rides together was a definite turn on. We flew to Europe and then traveled from city to city with Eurail passes, which gave us unlimited use of trains for the week we were on the ground. We also avoided the expense of hotels by booking compartments in sleeping cars. Using this somewhat unconventional mode of travel, we were able to hit five cities in five days: Oslo, Stockholm, Copenhagen, The Hague, and Brussels. In the process, we learned a great deal about the needs and priorities of potential donors. Indeed, our trip turned into a crash course in how to make yesable propositions to European funding agencies. To paraphrase Napoleon, we became engaged, and then we saw new possibilities—in this case, for future funding.

Probably the most important information we acquired was that the European Union (EU), the continent's largest donor, had an unwritten policy of rarely making grants to American NGOs. On learning this, we devised a relatively simple work-around. We reconfigured ourselves as Europeans, and we registered in Belgium as a nonprofit organization (*association sans but lucrative*) called the European Centre for Common Ground. Still needing to save money, we secured free office space and legal assistance from Hunton & Williams, a U.S. law firm with a Brussels office. Although we continued to be an American NGO headquartered in Washington, D.C., we legally became two organizations with a combined management structure.

Subsequently, most people we met in the EU understood that we were based in the United States, and we didn't try to conceal it. Nevertheless, we apparently were viewed to be sufficiently European to receive substantial EU support. In this and other ways, our chutzpah-laden, Eurail fundraising strategy clearly paid off. The EU became our largest single donor, and we received grants from the national governments of all five countries to which Susan and I traveled by train.

It was not only in fund-raising that we exhibited chutzpah. In developing new projects, we regularly pushed into areas where others had never before ventured. Sometimes that took a certain degree of nerve. Although we were often told that the time wasn't right for what we were proposing, we usually persisted. I realized that many people believe that the time is never right for adventurous new ideas. For example, in 1988 I had been sternly warned by a high State Department official not to take American participants to Moscow for a meeting of the U.S.-Soviet Task Force to Prevent Terrorism. The official who advised me to cease and desist held the rank of ambassador. As a former junior diplomat, I admit that I was somewhat intimidated by people who had reached such a high position in the State Department. In addition, as a common grounder, I was reluctant to get into a direct dispute with my own government. Rather than opposing official policy, I wanted to complement and enhance it. Also, I did not like the idea that I might be accused of being a *useful idiot* whom the Soviets were exploiting for propaganda purposes—which this ambassador was implying I was. Although those concerns were real, I went ahead anyway because both my gut and my mind told me that in those heady days of Gorbachev's reforms our initiative to promote cooperation against terrorism was timely and important. I had sufficient chutzpah to plow ahead.

Going against the warning from the ambassador was a calculated risk on my part. However, taking risks should not be confused with being foolhardy. As a social entrepreneur, I always tried to aim high—to shoot for the moon. But at the same time, I recognized that misfires were inevitable, and I came to see that aikido-type, small steps usually worked better than grand, unified solutions. In addition, whenever I was launching a risky project, I knew I could lessen the danger by taking preventive measures. For example, with the U.S.-Soviet Task Force to Prevent Terrorism, I assumed that opposition to our initiative was likely to come from the conservative side of the U.S. political spectrum, so I leaned to the right in selecting American participants. I also kept U.S. government officials informed about what I was doing, which became easier when the ambassador who had opposed the project was transferred to another post. Although I had nothing to do with his reassignment, it certainly was a stroke of good fortune. As a social entrepreneur, I did not underestimate the importance of being lucky.

Similarly, when we at Search were putting together our U.S.-Iran project, we were advised by another American ambassador—this one retired—that such a project might anger the administration and jeopardize future funding. Once again, we chose several conservative participants, and we made sure to keep government officials informed. We even persuaded the president of the United States to send a supportive message to participants at the first meeting. When we hit an obstacle with our policy proposals, we did not try to overwhelm the opposition, either in Washington, D.C. or in Tehran. In neither place would that have been an effective strategy. Rather, like the wind-up toy truck whose path is blocked by a piece of furniture, we backed off and found a way around. In the process, we invented *wrestling diplomacy* and made progress in ways that we had not anticipated when we began the project.

Despite our precautions, our U.S.-Iran project came up against an unforeseen obstacle—as the Dunbar Factor predicted it was likely to do. One of our Iranian colleagues, a distinguished Tehran University professor with whom we had been working closely for fourteen years, was stopped by customs officials as he entered the United States at Washington's Dulles Airport. Although he had a valid entry visa, he was led to a small room where FBI agents were waiting for hm. This was clearly not a spontaneous event where an alert customs agent had recognized that there might be a problem with his entry documents. The FBI men said that they wanted him to become their agent and to report on the activities of prominent

Iranian-Americans. They threatened him, stating that he would be indicted as an unregistered agent of the Iranian government if he failed to cooperate. However, if he agreed to work undercover, they said no charges would be filed against him, and he would not be deported from the United States. Faced with this unpalatable choice and unfamiliar with his rights under the American legal sysem, the professor came to us for help. We were clear that the charges were trumped up and that he was being prosecuted—and persecuted—because he had not agreed to spy for the FBI.

My colleagues and I were told by our lawyers that we, too, might be at risk if we assisted the professor. Our fears mounted when we were served with a federal subpoena—the only one we ever received in the history of the organization. We were required to turn over all of our records pertaining to the professor. Our lawyers told us that if federal officials could accuse our Iranian colleague of a crime, they might also claim that we were guilty of doing much the same thing—which we were in the sense that we had been collaborating with the professor to improve bilateral relations with Iran. Therefore, we could also be charged. We recognized that we had a legal obligation to comply with the subpoena, so we provided the government with copies of all of our documents that mentioned the professor, including reports of meetings and his travel records. Although we felt that there was nothing in the documents that damaged his case, we certainly did not like the idea of providing the government with accounts of our meetings and internal communications. In addition, our lawyers warned us that we might further incur the wrath of the FBI and the Justice Department if we persisted in helping the professor.

There was definitely chutzpah in our response. We were not about to leave a close colleague twisting slowly in the wind—particularly someone who we believed was innocent. The professor had risked both his career in Iran and reprisals from his own government to work with us. Our response was to find the professor *pro bono* legal representation and to provide him with a steady stream of advice—albeit not in direct meetings but through his lawyers and ours. By communicating through lawyers, we understood that our discussions were protected under attorney-client privilege. We considered taking the story of the FBI's heavy-handed approach to the media, but we decided not to do so because we didn't know whether publicity would help or hurt the case. In the end, our senior advisor, Ambassador (ret.) Bill Miller, accompanied by the professor's lawyer, had a long meeting with the U.S. attorney who was orchestrating the prosecution. Miller described in great detail the nature of what our Iranian colleague had been doing, and he explained that the professor's actions mirrored ours in seeking to improve the U.S.-Iran relationship. Because we weren't sure if the U.S. attorney understood the FBI's motivation, Miller also described what we regarded to be the coercive tactics the FBI had used to try to recruit the professor. For whatever reason, soon after this meeting the government dropped its main charge against the professor.

Our efforts to support the professor lasted more than two years. However, the time to make a decision about whether or not to aid him—which was our moment of truth—came after we first learned about the government's threat to prosecute him. As time progressed, the need for bold action—involving chutzpah—receded as our involvement became more routine and our initial fear of reprisal from the government lessened. With this case—and with most others—chutzpah was not a quality that was required to be displayed on a continuing basis.

The need for chutzpah can occur both at the beginning of a project and during the implementation stage, but it is usually called for only during a short period of time when a decision must be made, or when a corrective action is called for. After that point, the danger is likely either to become acute or to fade away.

11

Cultivate *Fingerspitzengefühl*

Reader beware! The principles of social entrepreneurship, as described in this book, are not cast in stone. They do not reflect received wisdom. They should be regarded as useful but not immutable. Although the list remained essentially the same throughout my entire career, on occasion I made additions and subtractions.

Perhaps the most notable add-on came after I gave a presentation to a group of European Searchers on what was then the list of principles. At the end, a Dutch colleague commented, "You left something out." I said that was entirely possible, and I asked her what was missing. She answered, "*Fingerspitzengefühl.*" She explained that this is a German word that literally means feeling through your fingertips. When people possess it, she said, they have an intuitive sense about a given situation and a spontaneous appreciation of how best to react. At the heart of *fingerspitzengefühl* is the innate ability to *know* without thinking.

Once I understood what the word meant, I realized that she was absolutely right. *Fingerspitzengefühl* was—and is—a crucial but immeasurable component of social entrepreneurship. Having a feeling for what should happen is a quality that can be extremely helpful. Novices starting out usually cannot successfully employ *fingerspitzengefühl*; social entrepreneurs enhance their ability to sense possibilities through extensive experience and deep immersion in their core activity. This is what one-time basketball star and later U.S. Senator Bill Bradley was referring to—albeit in a sporting context—when he said:

> When you have played basketball for a while, you don't need to look at the basket. . . . You develop a sense of where you are.

After being introduced to the concept of *fingerspitzengefühl*, I saw I had long been making use of it without realizing that the word even existed. This was another example of the phenomenon that Molière had in mind when he wrote, "For more than forty years, I have been speaking prose without knowing it."

When I compiled my first list of principles for social entrepreneurship, *fingerspitzengefühl* should have been included. However, I didn't know that I didn't know about it. Principle #11 of social entrepreneurship is "cultivate *fingerspitzengefühl*." The next time I made a presentation on social entrepreneurship, I added this principle to my list.

However, I recognized that social entrepreneurs need to exercise caution in applying *fingerspitzengefühl*. It is not a principle that should consistently be used to override a well-thought-out approach. Just as there is danger in social entrepreneurs—or anyone else—thinking they are the smartest people in the room, there is similar peril in making decisions based solely on instinct. Neither rational thinking nor intuitive impulses should be allowed to serve as the sole determinant in decision-making. Good decisions usually contain both empirical evidence *and* a positive answer to this question: Does it feel right?

In other words, social entrepreneurs should cultivate the ability to judiciously combine their intellect with their gut. I seemed to have accomplished this when, somewhat improbably, I brought the CIA and the KGB together to cooperate in preventing terrorism and also when I took American wrestlers to Iran. On other occasions I didn't listen to my instincts, and I sometimes made poor choices, which is what happened when I was approached in the year 2000 about setting up a Track 2 process between Americans and Libyans. Intuitively, this seemed like a great idea, but there were several logical reasons not to do it. One big one was that Muammar Qaddafi, then Libya's unquestioned ruler, appeared to have little inclination to change. In addition, I doubted that Search had the capacity to engage simultaneously with Iran and Libya, two countries widely considered to be outlaw states. I was very busy when the Libyan opportunity arose, and feeling overloaded certainly limited my openness to starting a new project. Nevertheless, if I had listened to my *fingerspitzengefühl*, I would have acted differently, but I allowed my rational mind to prevail.

With the benefit of hindsight, I believe I probably made the wrong decision, and as a consequence, we at Search missed a great opportunity. Unknown to us, Qaddafi would soon be looking to settle—or at least reduce—his differences with the United States. If my colleagues and I had launched a Track 2 Libyan-American initiative, I am reasonably sure that our efforts would have accentuated the change Qaddafi was on the brink of pursuing. This would have been yet another instance of riding a horse in the direction it was soon to be going. We would not have been trying to overcome historical trends, which is what we had been doing in our efforts to improve relations between Iran and the United States. With Libya, we would have been ahead of the curve, exactly where social entrepreneurs should position themselves.

In another instance, I followed my gut despite the fact that my rational self told me that getting involved would probably be the equivalent of hitting my head against a brick wall. The question at hand was abortion—inside the United States. This was a seemingly insoluble matter, and in the opinion of most people who supported us, it was not susceptible to the common ground approach. As mediation expert Michelle LeBaron has written:

> Even experienced conflict resolvers shrug their shoulders when the topic is raised, arguing that issues like abortion do not lend themselves to consensus building. After all, abortion is not a conflict in which proponents on either side are likely to change their views. The individuals involved are acting from deeply-held beliefs, values, conscience, and the sense that their views are, in fact, constitutionally protected rights.

In the early 1990s, then as now, the argument over abortion was harsh and polarized across the United States. Partisans on both sides confronted each other and consumed vast amounts of energy and resources. At the same time, other related problems—such as preventing unwanted pregnancies and improving maternal health—also required urgent attention. Unfortunately, the acrimonious battles around abortion greatly limited the country's ability to take constructive actions. The leaders of the two sides of the abortion debate were so angry with each other that they couldn't cooperate even in places where they agreed.

My impulse was to launch a project that brought together the pro-life and pro-choice camps to promote cooperation on issues related to abortion where there might be agreement. I felt this approach might work, even though there was virtually no evidence that it would—or should—be successful. Given the passion surrounding the abortion issue—plus the fact we at Search had virtually no experience working on hot-button, domestic matters—this was uncharted and possibly dangerous territory for us. Most of our supporters agreed that people in faraway places—such as Hutus and Tutsis or Israelis and Palestinians—should find common ground, but there was little agreement among Americans on either the right or the left that any accord could be found around abortion. On the level of rational analysis, the facts seemed to call for Search not getting involved. However, with the benefit of *fingerspitzengefühl*, my gut told me we should give it a try and launch a project.

Our involvement started in 1989 when we produced a TV program on abortion as part of our *Search for Common Ground* series that aired on U.S. public television. The guests were Kate Michelman, head of the National Abortion Rights Action League (NARAL), and John Willke, president of the National Right to Life Committee. Seeking common ground on abortion had enough of a man-bites-dog quality that the show attracted considerable attention.

Willke and Michelman profoundly disagreed with each other on the core question of abortion—yes or no. But using our format, which was based on the premise that their disagreement was only the starting point, the program moved on to a question rarely asked: Despite your massive differences, are there any related areas on which the pro-choice and pro-life camps might agree?

Michelman and Willke identified many such points. They agreed that both sides wanted to reduce the number of abortions (Willke wanted to take the number down to zero, whereas Michelman believed the option should be available as a matter of personal choice). They also were in agreement that unwanted pregnancies should be minimized; that promoting birth control was a point of common ground between many on both sides of the abortion issue (but not for these two); and that they could work together on efforts to promote adoption and reduce infant mortality. In addition, they both said that violence was never justified in support of their cause.

After watching a preview of our show, Christopher Lydon, WGBH-TV's lead anchor in Boston, narrated a segment describing it on his evening news broadcast. He referred to the involvement of Michelman and Willke thusly:

> By the end of the conversation, their body language and voice tones had all softened and the disarmed warriors were actually rushing to rack up points of agreement. . . . It looked almost if you had given them a pill.

Rest assured that we used no behavior-changing drugs. However, by asking different questions, different answers emerged.

From my perspective, our TV program proved that even bitter foes could find areas of agreement—not on the core question of whether abortion should be legal but on related matters, such as promoting adoption, minimizing the number of abortions in the United States, and ending violence around clinics. Furthermore, I believed that there was a substantial opening for a Search project to make these things happen because I felt that a large number of Americans did not hold absolute positions on abortion, and that the policies of organized groups on both sides often did not reflect popular opinion. I sensed that the country was ready for fresh approaches, and I thought some of the discordant energy around the abortion issue could be channeled in positive directions. I was not suggesting that the basic disagreement could be resolved or even bridged, but I felt that pro-choicers and pro-lifers could work together in ways that would produce both more choice and more life.

Moreover, if organizations on both sides cooperated to find ways to reduce the number of unwanted pregnancies, I believed there would be much less demand for abortions and that many fewer would take place. That, in turn, would probably lead to a reduction in polarizing rhetoric, and much of the poison would be drained from the national debate. If this were to happen, I recognized that there would almost certainly be opposition from groups on both sides of the issue—if for no other reason than a less poisonous atmosphere would probably lessen the urgency of both the pro-choice and pro-life causes and make it more difficult to raise funds. Above all, I had a strong sense that we at Search should go ahead.

The specific opportunity to do so emerged in 1992 as a direct, but unforeseen, result of our TV series. After the episode on abortion aired, we made the videotape widely available, and it was viewed by the leadership of the Buffalo, New York Council of Churches at a time of turmoil in that city over abortion. Operation Rescue, a militant pro-life group, had launched a highly controversial campaign to physically block access to local abortion clinics. In response, pro-choice activists had assembled on the streets to confront their foes and to keep the clinics open. The police wound up arresting 517 of the Operation Rescue supporters and eighteen of the pro-choice opposition. The Council of Churches, which included denominations with beliefs on both sides of the abortion issue, took it upon itself to try to defuse the conflict. At a certain point, the Council's director, the Reverend Stanford Bratton, sent me a letter in which he requested Search's assistance in reducing divisiveness. He wrote:

> It is our hope that you will help us move beyond our present situation toward the search for common ground and work on common issues identified in the process. We have used your videotape many times, and it has helped stimulate interest and hope here in Buffalo.

On receiving this letter, I moved quickly and flew from Moscow to Buffalo. Once there and on subsequent trips I worked with the Council of Churches to put together the Buffalo Coalition for Common Ground. It was governed by a fifteen-member Steering Committee balanced between pro-life and pro-choice partisans. Its mission statement declared it was committed to addressing the deep divisions that existed in the Buffalo area and the nation as a whole. As the *Chicago Tribune* later wrote about the Steering Committee's meetings:

> Discussions are respectful, but thorny. Moreover, participants often face hostility from members of their own movements who accuse them of negotiating with the enemy.

By virtue of establishing itself and agreeing to joint action, the Buffalo Coalition was modeling the very behavior that it aimed to establish in the larger community. The goal was to reframe the conflict in ways with which both pro-life and pro-choice participants could feel comfortable. Fundamental to the coalition and to our abortion-connected work elsewhere was the idea that no one was ever asked to change her or his belief about whether abortion should or should not be legal. Participants needed only to be willing to seek ways they could work together with people who held opposing views.

Around the same time that we started to work in Buffalo, local common ground groups spontaneously sprang up in St. Louis, San Francisco,

Milwaukee, and ten other cities. Emergence of these groups by no means represented a popular groundswell, but it was at least a budding trend. It showed that there might be an authentic base for a national organizing effort. As a result, we at Search contacted all the local groups we could identify and invited them to come to Washington, D.C. for a series of meetings. Under our auspices, their leaders agreed to form the Common Ground Network for Life and Choice. The network took on the mission of reducing polarization by encouraging dialogue and by helping to organize action-oriented projects.

During this period, we were able to raise a modest amount of money, and we hired two staff members, Adrienne Kaufmann and Mary Jacksteit, to lead the project. Kaufmann was a Catholic nun from the Benedictine order, and Jacksteit was a liberal attorney and mediator. They both had received master's degrees in conflict resolution. Because we probably could not have found a single staff member who would have been considered neutral on the question of abortion, the combination of these two seemed to represent a perfect pairing. Neither ever spoke of her personal stance, and both maintained impartiality. Although all of us who were connected to the project had our private views about abortion, our organization was never accused of favoring one side or the other.

Kaufmann's and Jacksteit's job was to furnish local groups with organizing assistance, program design, expertise on facilitation, training, and a quarterly newsletter. They carried out a series of meetings and dialogue sessions around the country, including three workshops for pro-choice and pro-life partisans in Buffalo. At first, participants were mainly interested in talking calmly with one another and exchanging personal stories. Most participants came to recognize that people on the other side were thoughtful individuals who usually had gone through painful experiences. In essence, these dialogue sessions allowed participants to rediscover their shared humanity. As *Harper's Magazine* reported, "The conversations were a positive, even transforming experience."

Many of the local groups moved on to implement joint projects. In some cities, pro-life and pro-choice members made appeals and appearances to reduce tensions and prevent violence. We held two national conferences that brought together the two sides. Commented one attendee:

> I have never listened so hard, been listened to so intently, never laughed and cried so hard. It reaffirms my commitment to love my opponent, something which can be lost in the heat of my activism.

We also commissioned and published a series of jointly written papers, including one coauthored by Karen Swallow Prior, a one-time Operation Rescue activist from Buffalo, and Marilyn Cohen, executive director of a women's health center in Iowa City that performed abortions. Both of these women were board members of our Network for Life and Choice, and they collaborated in writing a paper on setting standards for activism around abortion clinics. They affirmed support for nonviolence, free speech, and respect for women as moral decision-makers. They agreed that activists outside clinics should not use tactics that caused fear or intimidation; that women considering abortion should receive accurate, thorough, and objective information; and that pro-lifers and pro-choicers should be able to agree on information on fetal development and other scientific aspects of abortion.

We believed that the Network for Life and Choice was making real progress in defusing contentiousness and in giving Americans alternative ways to think about abortion. However, our efforts were regularly attacked from both the right and the left sides of the political spectrum. Interestingly, the Roman Catholic Bishop of Buffalo and a prominent liberal activist writing on the *New York Times* op-ed page used nearly identical language in declaring that common ground simply was not possible around abortion. Unfortunately, from our perspective, American foundations and donors proved unwilling to provide financial support to sustain the overall project. Potential funders turned out to be just as polarized as the activists who confronted each other in the streets, and they were not interested in supporting our consensus-building approach. Consequently, we were not able to raise enough money to keep the project going, and we were forced to close it in 1999 after six years of activity.

I still feel that the Network for Life and Choice was a much-needed initiative, and I have no regrets about having tried to build it into a national movement. If the ideas that underlaid it had taken hold, it would have made a huge impact. Obviously, we were trying to buck the rising tide of polarization. Unfortunately, to put it in figurative terms, we were riding a horse in the opposite direction from where it was going. My original feeling that we could make a success out of the Network for Life and Choice proved to be wrong.

Such is the problem with overreliance on *fingerspitzengefühl*. Sometimes it opens up the possibility that a social entrepreneur will move into a brave new world, and sometimes it does not.

12

Bringing It All Together

In the first eleven chapters, I have listed the principles of social entrepreneurship in a numerical progression—beginning with Principle #1 and moving numerically through to Principle #11. This is a logical way to present the principles, but in real life they are virtually never employed in such a neat sequence. Although Principle #1 (start from vision) and Principle #2 (be an applied visionary) are almost always put to use at the beginning of a venture, after that principles are used as needed and are not employed in any particular order. Some principles may be used repeatedly, and others simply may not be needed; but it is not unusual for all eleven principles to be part of a single initiative. This is exactly what happened in the following example, a project Search launched to improve relations between the United States and Syria.

Search's involvement began in 2006, three years before the Arab Spring led to civil war in Syria. At that time, a well-known Israeli journalist invited me and John Bell, a former Canadian diplomat who then headed Search's Middle East program, to lunch at the American Colony Hotel in Jerusalem. The journalist reminded us that the fifteenth anniversary of the Madrid Peace Conference was approaching, and he proposed we commemorate that event by cosponsoring with the Toledo International Center for Peace, a Spanish NGO, a conference to be called "Madrid 15 Years Later".

The original Madrid conference had taken place in 1991, thanks to the leadership of U.S. Secretary of State James Baker. For the first time ever, Israeli government officials, semiofficial Palestinians, and representatives of numerous Arab and Western governments came together in one official gathering. This landmark event had marked the beginning of unprecedented Middle East regional peace negotiations. As a direct result, four bilateral working groups involving Israel and its neighbors had been created, along with five multilateral groups that had dealt with issues including water, environment, arms control, refugees, and economic development. Although no final agreements were reached and the process had petered out after a few years, these negotiations in Madrid had gone further toward resolving regional conflict than any previous effort.

Fifteen years later, the prospects for peace in the region had regressed. The Israeli journalist's vision, which we Searchers realized we shared, was to relaunch a comprehensive Middle East peace process (Principle #1: start from vision). To give life to this vision, the journalist proposed that we and the Toledo Center convene a reunion event in Madrid that would bring together high-level, unofficial representatives of the regional and international countries that had participated in the original conference (Principle #2: be an applied visionary).

The journalist planned to cover the conference. He was not interested in organizing it, but he wanted it to happen. He believed that having an American and a Spanish NGO as the principal sponsors would be a good way to establish a safe space for bringing together prominent Israelis and Arabs. He chose us to be the American group because he knew we had been showing up in the Middle East for the last sixteen years (Principle #4: keep showing up), so he offered us this opportunity on a silver platter. We had proved to his satisfaction that we could successfully bring together well-placed Israelis and Arabs.

We said "yes" to the journalist's proposal, and we listened attentively to what he thought such a conference might look like. He had anticipated many of the details, and we accepted most of his ideas. However, when it came to paying for the gathering, what he suggested turned out to be a bridge too far. To finance the proceedings, he offered to introduce us to a rich American hedge fund operator who he said was interested in supporting the event. We were appalled at the idea of taking money from this man because we knew he was under indictment in the United States for serious crimes and had fled to Switzerland to avoid prosecution. Even though there would have been nothing illegal about our receiving a sizable contribution, we stated that we did not want to be associated with someone with this sort of record. Accepting this money would not have passed what we called the Washington Post test. In other words, we would not have liked to read in our morning newspaper that this individual had paid for the conference. We said we would be glad to play a key role in organizing the event, but we would need to find other sources of funding. In the end, that did not prove to be too difficult, and we were able to work with the Toledo Center to secure grants from the Spanish, Swedish, Norwegian, and Danish governments.

We Searchers ordinarily took pride in designing meetings with creative formats that led to concrete action. For the Madrid conference, however, we realized we would need something different from our norm. After all, this would be a one-shot affair, and its main value would be to demonstrate that there was still a high level of interest in Middle East peacemaking. We expected to have more than one hundred attendees, who would include a former president, three former prime ministers, and twelve current or former foreign ministers.

We surmised that many of the attendees would not be comfortable with anything participatory or unorthodox. Individuals like these were used to delivering speeches, and they tended to be less interested in listening and interacting with others. Therefore, we worked closely with the Toledo Center to put together a conference that had a traditional, set-piece format. There was no third-party facilitation and little informality. The action was to be in the corridors during coffee breaks and in small meetings held in hotel rooms. Rather than following our usual practice of hosting participants in informal dinners with plenty of wine on the table, the Toledo Center arranged for the King and Queen of Spain to invite everyone over to the palace for a formal reception.

As we planned the conference, the big unknown was whether a Syrian delegation would attend. We felt Syria was vital to creating peace in the Middle East, but its leaders seemed to have an allergy to Track 2 gatherings—a condition to which we at Search had contributed thirteen years earlier when we had sponsored unofficial talks between Syrians and Israelis and the story had leaked to the press. As Bouthaina Shaaban, a key advisor to President Bashar al-Assad, later told one of my colleagues, "We thought we—a strong centralized state—didn't need any help from civil society. Plus, the Foreign Ministry felt [there was] competition from nonofficial talks."

To our great relief, at the last minute we received word that Syrians would be coming to the conference and their delegation would be led by Riad Daoudi, the director of the Judicial Department of the Syrian Presidency and a legal advisor to the Ministry of Foreign Affairs. My colleagues and I were familiar with him because he had been a top negotiator for the Syrian government for many years. Although our conference was supposedly an unofficial gathering, we were pleased that the Syrian regime decided to send someone with impressive official credentials. That meant, in our view, that the Assad regime was taking our gathering somewhat seriously.

At the conference itself, I happened to be seated on the dais only a few feet away from Daoudi. During one of the breaks, I walked over and introduced myself. He knew exactly who I was, and he mentioned my role in the Track 2 talks Search had previously sponsored between Syrians and Israelis. Our conversation was cordial, and Daoudi seemed open to engagement. Soon we were calling each other "Riad" and "John." We lamented the extent to which Syrian-American relations had deteriorated in the post-9/11 world after the George W. Bush administration had made clear that it was the American way or the highway. Impulsively, I suggested to Daoudi that Track 2 meetings might be able to produce a blueprint on how to improve things (Principle #11: cultivate *fingerspitzengefühl*). He seemed favorable to the idea, but he said he would have to check with Damascus before he could make a commitment.

It took several months for Daoudi to get back to me with a green light from the Syrian Foreign Ministry and presumably from President Assad himself. Unfortunately, the Madrid 15 Years Later conference did not achieve the vision that had originally motivated us, and no meaningful new negotiations followed. But our engagement did lead to something constructive—the emergence of a new, unofficial U.S.-Syrian Working Group (Principle #3: on s'engage, et puis on voit).

Once Daoudi and the Syrians agreed to participate, my colleagues and I were able to secure funding for the Working Group from the Norwegian government. To work out the agenda, I headed off to Damascus, joined by Sam Lewis, the longtime U.S. Ambassador to Israel, and Rob Malley, then of the International Conflict Group and more recently President Biden's emissary for Iran nuclear talks (Principle #5: enroll credible supporters).

We met with Daoudi and agreed that the Working Group would seek to "normalize relations between Syria and the United States by bringing together influential people from both countries to formulate strategies to help overcome current barriers."

The first meeting of the Working Group took place in May 2007 in Damascus. To the American delegation we added Steve Bartlett, a former Republican congressman who had also been mayor of Dallas, and Theodore Kattouf, a former U.S. ambassador to Syria (Principle #5 again: enroll credible supporters). My wife, Susan Collin Marks, facilitated the meetings, as she had previously done with our Iranian-American sessions. Although our group was supposedly nonofficial, a notetaker from the Syrian Foreign Ministry was present for each session, and the foreign minister himself kept telephoning a Syrian participant during the group's working sessions. These calls were made, of course, in Arabic, but the Syrian who received them stayed in the room while he talked on his cell phone. Thanks to one of our American participants who understood Arabic, we received a briefing on what was said after each session. The foreign minister clearly was interested in what we were doing, and these calls confirmed that the Syrian government at the top level was providing direction to our Syrian participants. Due to Foreign Ministry involvement, we described the meeting as Track 1.5.

When the first session began, the Syrian and American participants automatically took seats on opposite sides of the table. This was the normal seating arrangement in binational gatherings. Susan sat at the head of the table and asked participants to sit next to someone from the other country. In this way, instead of participants facing each other as adversaries, which was largely the way Syria and the United States were then relating to each other, participants sat together and took on a shared problem: How to have better relations between the two countries.

The results of this first meeting were modest but promising. Participants declared that they wanted to continue the process and said they would gladly attend future sessions. They agreed to convey the results back to their respective governments and to urge them to allow more access and freer movement for diplomats and journalists. In addition, Sami Moubayed, a Syrian historian and writer, and Ambassador Theodore Kattouf were tasked with coauthoring two articles on "What's the Common Ground between the U.S. and Syria on Iraqi refugees?" Their work with a shared byline was subsequently published in *Al Hayat*, arguably the Arab